Powerful Presentation Principles

52 Presenting Rules to Help You Prepare, Present and Persuade

Paula Smith

Copyright © Paula Smith
Published by Allsouth Pty Ltd
Edited by Jonquil Brooks, Brick Cat Editing
Design and Layout by Sarah Taylor-Smith
First Published 2014
First Edition
ISBN 9780980725612

ACKNOWLEDGEMENTS

To my precious family and friends.
Here's to the remarkable life I have because
you are in it. Feeling loved and wanted by you
all is everything I could ever wish for.

To my speaker buddies and clients. You are an
extension of my family. My tribe. I am so very grateful
for every piece of advice you have given, support you have
shown and experiences we have shared together.

You all rock!

PRINCIPLES

INTRODUCTION

It is my belief that anyone can be a presenter. Are presenters born or made? Definitely made.

We all know someone who appears to be able to capture the audience every time they speak or can jump up at a moment's notice and give an impromptu speech. Although this may seem like a natural gift and their ability to engage and entertain may be quite incredible, their charismatic charm doesn't necessarily make them a powerful presenter.

A powerful presenter not only engages and entertains but has consciously and deliberately designed and delivered their message with specific outcomes and results in mind. A presentation that inspires others to take positive action is a powerful presentation. A presentation that empowers others to change behaviour is a powerful presentation. A presentation that emotionally moves others to believe in themselves is a powerful presentation.

Presenting is both art and science and to be a powerful presenter you can learn and master both.

Presentation skills are one of the most profitable skills you can learn in modern business. Being able to engage your audience and get your message across is a vital communication skill. Whether it is to an audience of 1 or 1,000 the ability to prepare, present and persuade is an essential life and business skill.

There are 52 presenting principles in the pages before you, one for every week of the year. The only way to get better at presenting is to present. Don't try to master all 52 in your first or next presentation. Take your time and little by little move out of your comfort zone and try to take a few risks one step at a time. Not every principle will be relevant for every presentation so ensure you choose appropriately on each occasion.

The 52 principles are shared directly from my own experience as a professional speaker and trainer along with the expertise and advice from some of the most recognised names in the speaking industry. I hope they give you the insight and skills you need to be able to step up to the platform to be that engaging expert you aspire to be.

I wish you every presenting success.

Paula

START WITH THE END IN MIND

Preparation, preparation, preparation

Every presentation starts with a need – a need to inspire, motivate and change behaviour. A presenter then has an idea – an idea of how their message will achieve this.

Unfortunately, all too often their idea, their spark of brilliance, their key message, is lost because of poor, or a lack of, preparation and design.

Successful presenters understand that most of the work that goes into a powerful presentation is essentially off the platform.

I have seen many a presenter/trainer/speaker sit at their desk and open their slideshow software as their presentation planning method.

Stop! This is one of the last items on the design agenda.

First, consult with all the key stakeholders. Decide together what the purpose of this presentation is and agree on the outcome and objectives.

Then access a very thorough presentation checklist and ensure you spend enough time, energy and resources on even the smallest of details.

A good place to start is the:

Who?

What?

Where?

When?

Why?

Construct your own presentation checklist and use it every time you or someone in your organisation needs to start the planning process.

Then, when you get to "HOW am I going to achieve these outcomes and get my message across effectively", read through the next 51 presentation rules.

Don't ever try to wing a presentation. I know it may work once or twice but you are gambling with the time, money and potential success of your audience or your client. Respect everyone and 'plan' to make your presentation count.

DELIVER AN OPENING TO REMEMBER

Get attention and incite curiosity

"Did you know?"

"You would never believe what happened to me this morning."

"83% of everyone in this room will suffer from ..."

"A life with no beer."

"Imagine if you woke up one morning and ..."

"By the close of business today another 350 small business owners will close their doors forever and file for bankruptcy."

These are all examples of presentation openings. Did you notice that not one of them sounded like "Good morning, my name is Paula Smith and I am going to talk to you about..."

The opening and closing of your presentation are the most powerful elements of a presentation.

Your opening should be designed to get attention and incite curiosity, to ensure the audience wants to hear more and to get them into the state of the moment.

Not all openings have to be words or even have shock value. You may choose to show an image, play a video clip or roller skate across the stage (okay, this may shock some of the audience).

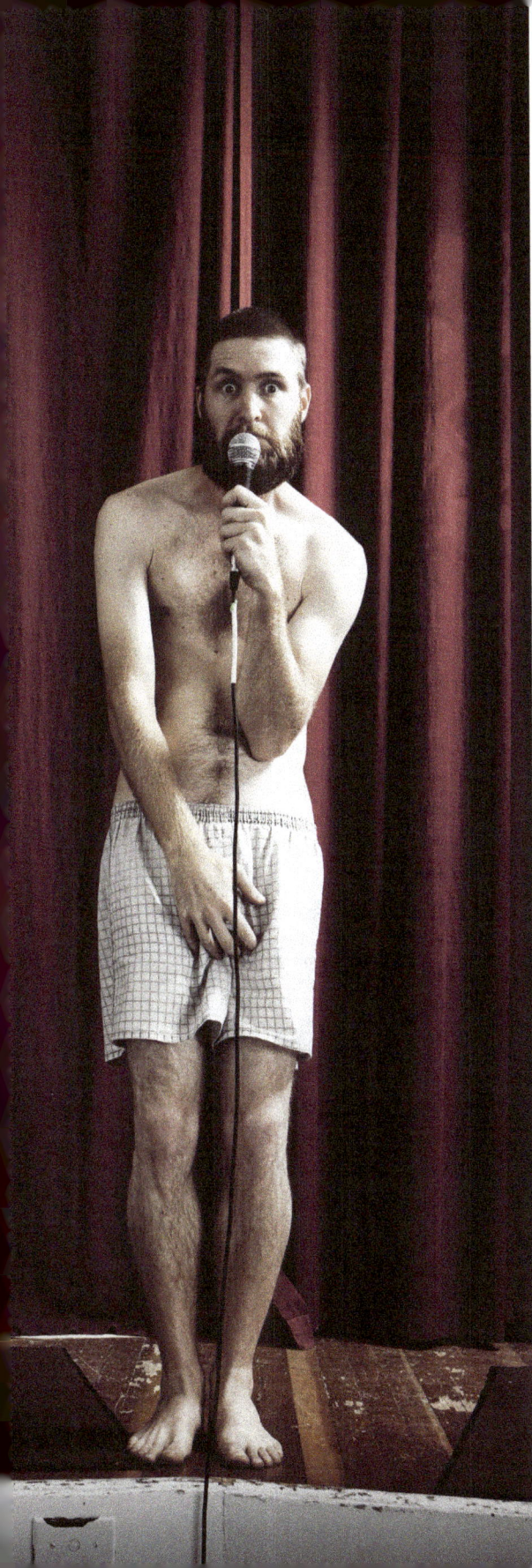

Your opening should be powerful and relevant (even if the relevance isn't obvious immediately).

Even where you are in the room will make a huge difference to how powerful your opening is. If you are delivering words as your opening and you are on the platform, ensure you stand still and deliver centre stage. You could even start with a voice in the dark before the stage lights shine on you. If your image on a screen is the opening, move to one side and let the image take centre stage.

Your opening could be a story, a piece of music, a statistic, a powerful proverb or an action. Whatever you choose as your opening, never open a presentation again with "Good morning, my name is ...", because that is exactly what the audience expects.

Step up, stand out and make an entrance. The audience will then be alert, present and ready for you and your message.

DELIVER A CLOSING TO REMEMBER

And get results

You may now have a great idea for your opening. That's awesome but when planning your creative opening plan your closing at the same time.

Your closing must also be as powerful as your opening.

Your closing will be the last thing people hear from your presentation. Never finish by saying: "That's it. Do you have any questions?" You have no control of what questions will be asked. If someone is annoyed with something you have said or they ask something not quite relevant to your intended message, this may end up being the conversation in the hallway after your presentation. Question and Answer time is important but not at this critical point in your presentation.

You need to be in control of the message and the emotional state you leave your audience in.

Many experienced presenters link their opening with their closing. For example, "Imagine if you woke up this morning and..." was the opening. Now you can close with, "We imagined what this morning could look like – now you don't need to imagine any more as tomorrow morning this could be your reality".

"350 small business owners filed for bankruptcy yesterday. There is no need for you to become another failed small business statistic."

If you opened with a excerpt from a video perhaps play the same video but this time let the video keep running and reveal the happy ending.

Keep in mind that if you started centre stage, finish centre stage. You have already anchored in the memory of your audience that powerful things happen centre stage.

The law of primacy and recency suggests we always remember the first and last things we see and hear. Ensure your audience sees and hears exactly what you intended them to.

BE A THOUGHT LEADER

Bring fresh insights

"How was the presentation?" "Okay. Nothing I haven't heard before."

Sound familiar?

I go to a lot of presentations as I am sure many of you do too. Which ones stand out? Which ones have you thinking in a way you have never thought before? Which ones aroused your emotions or got you to take action for the very first time?

Why do some presenters get booked over and over again?

Anyone with a bit of training can deliver a presentation that sounds professional and gets the job done.

The world-class presenters are thought leaders. They bring something unique to the platform – a different take on a topic, breakthrough research, their own models and frameworks. They are thought leaders.

Thought leaders are critical thinkers, they challenge assumptions, and take notice of their own thinking. When they are in flow they are captivating.

When we attend a presentation and hear something unique or innovative we talk about it, we assess our own thoughts and feelings about it and we are sometimes more influenced to give something this different a try.

Research also suggests that when we hear or experience something for the first time, our emotional state is stimulated and we are more likely to remember it.

So have something interesting to say. When you choose a piece of content to include in your presentation, say to yourself:

"What is this and can this be useful for this presentation?"

"What do I think about this?"

"What are the possibilities?"

Create your own thoughts to share, create your own IP (intellectual property). Create a presentation to be talked about.

Become a thought leader.

NOT EVERYONE WILL LIKE WHAT YOU HAVE TO SAY

Make a stand

As a person who takes the platform, the training room or the board room floor you must be prepared to accept that not everyone is going to like or agree with what you have to say.

If you just plan a presentation with what everyone wants to hear, to ensure everyone will like you and to not make any waves, your presentation will be what my husband describes as 'beige'. I like purple, I love red, I choose to try blue on occasion and sometimes I throw in a little bit of black. Most of the time though it's a bright rainbow of colour being splashed around – that's what I plan. I would never plan to be beige.

"If you stand for something, you will always find some people for you and some against you. If you stand for nothing, you will find nobody against you, and nobody for you."

–Bill Bernbach

I love this quote. Bill Bernbach was the creative powerhouse at the advertising agency Doyle Dane Bernbach and one of the most influential people in advertising history. Bernbach was known for his devotion to creativity and offbeat themes, a legacy that has credited him as a major force behind the creative revolution of the 1960s and 1970s. He always stood for something.

The reason you may have been asked to speak is because you do have a unique perspective on things. You may have been recognised as a thought leader in your industry or maybe you do have the knack of bringing controversy to a conference and that is exactly what is needed to shake things up a little.

Take a risk, have the courage to stand for something. Believe in your presentation and your message even when it's being questioned.

Accept that not every audience is the right audience for you.

Be known for something rather than not being known for anything.

Don't plan to be a beige presenter, choose your palette and stand by it.

GET THE AUDIENCE ON YOUR SIDE

Be confident but not arrogant

In your first moments on the platform the audience, just like in any other introduction, will form a first impression. And we all know first impressions can be lasting.

It helps if the audience is on your side right from the beginning. This is different to the previous point about not designing your presentation so that everyone agrees with you about everything. This is about gaining respect and trust from the audience before you have the right to challenge anyone's values or belief system. If you show respect for your audience they will in turn give you the respect you deserve to share your views.

In so many presentations I have seen the presenter, during the first few lines, make unjustified comments based on their narrow-minded assumptions, insult half the audience in what they thought was a great opening joke, move on to criticising the industry or their organisation, and then expect the audience to be warm and welcoming.

If you get the audience offside, you have lost much of your influencing power.

A presenter who does not seek respect from their audience is, in my opinion, just arrogant.

Confidence is different to arrogance. Aim to be confident with your views and, if presenting facts, bring evidence to back your claims, but be mindful that your audience may have strong views too and may need a little more convincing. If they dislike you or have no respect for you, you will be fighting an uphill battle to the end.

So ask yourself the question: Are you a confident or an arrogant speaker?

A confident speaker:

- cares about what their audience will take away from the session
- rehearses to ensure they are at their best
- finds out what the client really needs
- is open to adapting their style and presentation to suit the target group including interactive activities or Q and A
- welcomes a continuous relationship with participants or clients
- actively sources feedback after the event and discusses evaluation strategies to measure effectiveness.

An arrogant speaker sounds like this:

- "Doesn't worry me if they don't do anything with the information – I still get paid."
- "I've done this same presentation 10 times over, no need to rehearse anything, it's a breeze."
- "No I don't customise presentations, I have put a lot of work into my content and my PowerPoint, it will ruin it."
- "Questions? No questions, just in case they challenge anything I have just told them."
- "Sorry, what was that? How will we evaluate? Oh no need, I've done this before, I'll be great."

Your attendees will talk about you and your presentation. Be talked about for all the right reasons.

DON'T TALK TO STRANGERS

Mum was right

Mum said "Don't talk to strangers." She was right!

I know all business is about relationships and to build a relationship with people we do have to meet new people, but in a presentation I repeat myself: never ever talk to strangers.

A stranger is someone you don't know. A 'Stranger Audience' is an audience you know nothing about, so how can you be confident you are sharing the right message for them?

You must aim to find out as much as possible about every audience member before you take the platform.

If you don't know who you are speaking to you end up with a second rate presentation designed for everyone that makes not a lot of difference to anyone.

Some facts you may want to find out include:

- ✓ Gender mix
- ✓ Age group
- ✓ Previous experiences (even which speaker they had last year)
- ✓ Lifestyle
- ✓ Career paths
- ✓ Current issues
- ✓ Past issues
- ✓ The people in their life
- ✓ Promises made about this event.

If you have a smaller group you can take time to do a little more research. My colleagues used to laugh at me when I would Google all of my participants before a workshop. It still amazes me what I can find out about a person when I do an internet search. I don't do it to be nosey either (okay, sometimes I do), I research so I can start working on some potential solutions for clients before the workshop even begins. Your audience is sometimes quite surprised and impressed about how much you do know about them.

The more information you can find out about the audience before the presentation the more you can contextualise the presentation to ensure your participants receive real value. It also gives you many points of connection.

This is a simple thing to do that demonstrates your commitment and investment to the success of the event.

So proudly announce to the person booking you that you never talk to strangers.

BE AN ENGAGING EXPERT

The brain doesn't remember boring things

The million dollar question is: "What does it take to be a great speaker?"

The quickest answer I can give you is: "Be an engaging expert."

There are many people out there who claim to be an expert in their field, and there are many people out there who claim they can speak on just about anything and be engaging.

The trick is to be able to be both.

We can all relate to sitting in a conference where we have had an academic professor presenting the latest research in their field. Mind blowing research that could change the world forever and for a moment we were compelled to hang onto every word but as the 76th slide rolls over (not that we can read the size 12 font on the slide anyway) we find our minds shifting to that glass of red waiting for us at the end of the day. Yes, some presentations may cause us to start drinking.

So, what if a brilliant mind presented cutting edge material in an innovative, entertaining and completely engaging manner? So engaging, in fact, we listened to the very end and clearly received the intended message of the presentation.

It doesn't sound that difficult does it? It really is just great content presented in a way which isn't boring.

Now speaking of boring, according to John Medina's book *Brain Rules*, we do not remember boring things. Audiences check out after about 10 minutes. Emotional arousal throughout your presentation, not more tables that they can't read, helps the brain to stay awake and not get bored. You can grab them back every 10 minutes by telling narratives or creating events rich in emotion. The boring presenter stuck with their notes behind a lectern loses their participants early in the delivery and, unfortunately, keeps going to the bitter end and never manages to get them back. What a waste of an opportunity.

So ask yourself these two questions:

1. Am I an expert in the content/topic I am presenting? (Remember, being an expert is also linked to perception – the mere fact that you may have had a firsthand experience in something, such as climbing a mountain, may be enough for you to be positioned as a person with sought-after expertise.)

2. Are my presentations really engaging? Am I engaging? You may need to ask an honest mentor, client or friend this question.

Master both to claim you are truly an engaging expert.

PRESENTATION PURPOSE

What is the purpose of your presentation?

Presenters who choose to stand up and speak out should have one primary purpose: to get their message across.

There are many ways a presenter can do this; however, before the presenter can prepare a presentation they need to be very clear about the purpose of their presentation.

Is the purpose to inform or educate?
(Give some facts, demonstrate a skill, present some statistics)

Is the purpose to entertain?
(Share some stories, audience interaction, add some humour)

Is the purpose to influence or persuade?
(Move to action, share social proof, benefits of change)

Is the purpose to award or reward (ceremonial)?
(Toast to the bride and groom, presenting an award, stating accolades)

Every presentation will be a different combination of all of the above depending on the very clear message you wish to communicate, the action you wish your audience to take and the length of the presentation or training.

For example, an after dinner presentation may be 60% entertain, 20% influence and 20% inform. An educational one-day session may be 60% inform, 30% entertain and 10% influence. It could be a sales presentation: 20% inform, 20% entertain and 60% influence. Or a wedding speech could be made up of 5% inform, 40% entertain, 5% influence, 50% ceremonial.

Once you know your purpose, it makes the planning and preparation of your presentation much easier as you can consciously and deliberately insert key messages and actions in the right places in the presentation.

So choose your presentation recipe to ensure maximum effectiveness.

WHY ARE WE HERE?

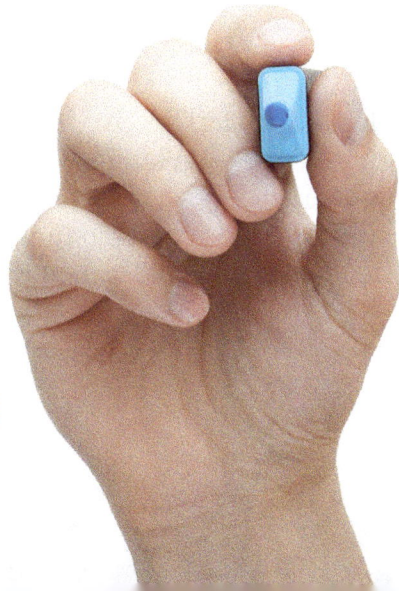

DON'T BE TOO CLEVER WITH YOUR PRESENTATION TITLE

You've got them in the door, make sure they want to stay

Your presentation title must reflect what you are delivering.

Just like at the beginning of a presentation, you do need to get attention and incite curiosity; however, you need to ensure if they buy into the title they will be rewarded with content that meets or exceeds their expectations.

It's like a great book: it has a title that makes you look twice, it draws you in to reading the tag line to see if it's the type of book you are interested in reading, then perhaps you will flick through the pages to see if it meets a need or solves a problem you are facing. If what is inside does not reflect the title and the tag line, it goes back on the shelf.

In a presentation, that could mean a very unhappy client or, worse still, a walk out.

People will feel deceived, as though you have misled them in some way. Trust is everything in a presentation, don't ever fool someone into attending your presentation or workshop. If they don't trust you they will be resisting any ideas you put forward and your influencing ability could be non-existent.

The trick is to align the content with a presentation title that gets an instant reaction. The tag line is another one or two lines that explains what problems you can solve or how you can help them. For example, a book by Joan Barker, *Live the Dream – Become rich and free through your business.* Or a friend of mine has a book titled *Brain Fit – How smarter thinking can save your brain.*

Go for a walk through your bookstore and look at all the great titles for inspiration or even flick through your daily newspaper. The media use the same strategies to engage us. Great headline, then the next line tells you a little more about what's to come in the story so you will read on. If it's not what you were promised, you turn the page.

Advertisers and marketers also use a similar strategy.

You can be clever when clever is called for though. You can play around with famous sayings, books, songs and quotes and replace one or more of the words with your content.

I did this with my first book: **Speaking** in the Shower instead of **singing,** and one of the programmes I deliver is Make Money While you **Speak,** instead of **sleep.**

Your title also has to evolve to meet the current market. For example, 25 years ago I was delivering workshops on 'professional image'. Then people didn't buy professional image any more, they were buying a workshop on personal branding – same principles in the workshop, different title. Then personal branding was getting a bit stale, clients wanted cutting edge material so the title and, of course, some of the content was re-marketed as reputation management. Off and running again. Have you got some old tired titles that could be re-branded and re-marketed?

Having a great presentation title is only part of your marketing strategy to get people in the door and bums on seats – you just want to make sure that they are more than happy to keep their bottoms there until the very end.

A STRUCTURE WILL SET YOU FREE

7 steps to presentation success

If you think a structure is restrictive and won't let you speak off the cuff or adapt your presentation for the target audience, think again.

A good solid presentation structure will really set you free. If you use a proven successful structure your presentation will flow, your planning becomes easy and you will look and sound like a professional every time.

In my first book I revealed the 7 Steps to Presentation Success.

The structure is based on my 25 or more years of experience working with trainers and professional speakers and even teaching children how to stand up and speak out with confidence.

World-class presenters make it look easy. It is easy for them because they understand the art and science of presenting so they know exactly when, where and how to place critical messages throughout the presentation. When you have sound structure it takes hours of planning time off your busy schedule.

Your presentation is like a big jigsaw puzzle. Starting with the framework makes putting in all the other pieces of the puzzle so much quicker and easier.

Your 7 steps to presentation success.

1.   Guess What
(Get attention and incite curiosity.)

Read Principle Number 2. Deliver an opening to remember.

2.   Why Me?
(This is who I am, this is why I am here. Credibility statement.)

Read Principle Number 17. Craft your credibility statement

3.   Why You?
(This is all about you the audience, this is how I can help you. Key message.)

Read all 52 principles. The audience is there for WIIFM (what's in it for me). Every presentation should be audience-centred. We sometimes have to clearly state in this section why they are here and the benefits of attending.

4.   The Destination
(This is where we are going and how we are going to get there.)

There is always a portion of the audience who want to know exactly what their day or the next hour will look like. Questions such as: When do we have our breaks? Can we ask questions? What do we do with the workbooks? How long will this take? Will there be handouts? Will I be expected to do anything? This is when presenters let the audience know exactly what to expect during the presentation and what you are expecting of them. Some audience members really don't care if you don't tell them anything but remember, it's about the whole audience on your side. And many people, unfortunately, just don't receive surprises very well at all.

5.   The Journey
(The information you are going to share with the audience.)

The first four steps of this structure will set the framework and boundaries for the whole presentation. If you get steps 1–4 right the audience will be ready to receive you and your presentation and all it has to offer.

This is where you get the chance to educate, inform, persuade, inspire, entertain and motivate through offering and sharing your expertise and experience.

Remember to read through the principles about how to ensure your message is received, remembered and actioned.

6.   The Relationship
(I am interested in you. What else can I do for you?)

When the presentation is over we need to thank the audience or state what a pleasure it was to be speaking to them. This is also the time we can let the audience know where they can find out more about you or more information about the content. It is a time to let the audience know you do care about them and the outcomes of the presentation. Many people who sell from stage will pitch their sale here too.

7.   The Arrival
(Action, powerful close, key message.)

Read Principle number 3. To get results, deliver a closing to remember.

It's time to go. Before you do you must ask the audience to take action. The action you intended them to take or the behaviour you intended them to change as a result of your words.

The key messages of the presentation need to be reinforced during the arrival.

Delivering the opening and closing are critical parts of your structure. Both must be powerful. I always try to link my closing with my opening too in some way. I can do this by finishing the opening story, repeating my opening and now making it relevant to the action I wish them to take or even by finishing in the same location on the stage as where I started from. This location has now been anchored in their minds as an important place I go to share powerful messages.

You may not use a structure and wing it. If you wing it, it will be hit and miss. I would never want to invest in a hit-and-miss presenter. It is too much of a risk.

Be consistently great. Using a structure sets you free so you can be confident of delivering presentation success every time.

CONTENT IS KING

And sometimes queen

You may have heard the expression "Content is king" but, as I have explained in previous principles, content delivered badly is definitely not presentation royalty.

When I have been asked to help find a keynote for a conference or a trainer for the day most people ask for someone who is an expert in their field. Not surprising at all. The next question I get asked is, "Have I seen them present?" If the answer is "no" my recommendation loses weight very quickly. We all know a lot of experts, people who have the expertise we are looking for, but what we need is that "engaging expert" – a presenter who knows how to deliver their content and also be able to connect to the audience. A presenter who can explain complex theories by using simple models or metaphors. A presenter who can contextualise their content to make it relevant to every person in the room.

Many conference organisers, meeting planners or clients want someone with expertise who can get their message across so will decide to book the number 2 or 3 expert or guru because of their ability to engage and entertain the audience as well.

Content is not always king. It sometimes has to play queen so the king of speaking and presenting can take the throne.

A king with no substance can be overthrown very quickly though. A king with fresh insight, leadership, authenticity, an ability to connect with their kingdom and some pretty awesome content really is "presentation royalty".

May I also convince you they will be rewarded with the respect of their subjects and will get paid in riches you can only dream about (also known as a high speaking fee).

Are you ready to be crowned?

THE NOW PRESENTATION

Make money, save money, save time and be happier now

The difference between children and adults in a learning environment is that a child usually accepts the method of teacher-directed learning. This is what we are going to learn today whether you want to or not because it's in the curriculum.

One of the principles for adult learning is that adults insist on relevance. Can I use this knowledge or skill in my life or workplace now or in the not-so-distant future?

I coach a lot of emerging speakers: speakers who have a great message for the world, and want to turn what they know – their expertise – into a business. Speakers who want to be able to adapt their message for a commercial market.

One of the first questions I ask them is: "If I was CEO of an organisation how would your message either make me money, save me money or save me time?"

Your message or your presentation must be relevant to your target market and their current issues. Lots of topics are interesting and may even have the wow factor but would I pay for them?

Many presenters have brilliant content and innovative ideas but to any organisation that has very clear outcomes and a strict budget they may just state: So what! Who cares!

Remember, an organisation will ask these questions:

Will this presentation solve a current problem?

Will this presentation make me money or save me money?

Will this presentation help me or my staff be more productive?

Is this presentation relevant?

Even an individual attending your public workshop is looking for answers to a problem they may be experiencing now. They may want to be slimmer, richer or happier.

If you have a keynote you are known for, you can still contextualise it to make it relevant right now for this group of people, in this organisation.

People want NOW presentations – 'sometime later' or 'for someone else' is not always an easy sell.

14

KEY MESSAGES THAT STICK

Getting your message remembered

Let me be very clear about this one. You have one purpose in a presentation: to get your message across.

However, we must ensure that our message sticks.

In the planning stages of our presentation we must be very clear of what our key messages are. A key message is "what do I want my audience to leave with, or what behaviours do I want them to change as a result of my message". In fact, your audience should be able to easily recall your key message when sharing with others what the presentation was all about.

I always suggest one or three key messages that you can leave them with are the most powerful.

Why one or three? It's easy to remember one message as this can be in your opening, reiterated throughout your presentation and of course your final message in your closing. The rule of primacy and recency suggests we will always remember the first and last things we see and hear. We tend to remember first events and last events too.

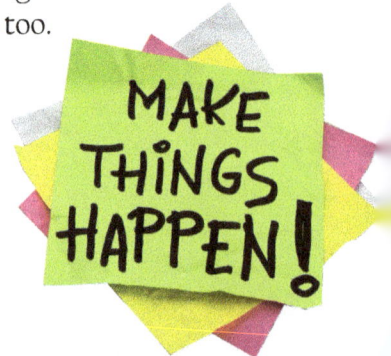

MAKE THINGS HAPPEN!

Episodic memory, which is the memory of autobiographical events, assists us in travelling back in time to remember events in order.

I bet you can remember your first day at school and the last day of school? I doubt you would remember your 5th day of school (unless a major event happened on this day).

Just like you can remember what you had for breakfast today but you would probably struggle to remember what you had 10 days ago. But you may remember the first breakfast you ever had in your new home.

Can you make a first event for your audience? The first time they have heard this concept, the first time they have heard this catch phrase.

So why three key messages and not two? Have you heard of the rule of three? Tricolon is the more formal term. We tend to remember things in sets of three.

Even storytellers and marketers use this theory. Three bears, three little pigs, three musketeers, even Donald Duck has three nephews and we can remember all of them. The skin cancer foundation's iconic and internationally recognised campaign Slip, Slop, Slap, for example, was embedded in all Australians' psyche. You can even use a tricolon to increase the intensity of a message and help people remember it. I need you to see, I need you to feel, I need you to be completely immersed.

Things that we say in threes are also easier to remember because they are rhythmic. We even count in threes. How many times did you say to your children, "I will count to three, and then...".

Later in the book, we cover many other ways to help embed messages. Remember, a message that isn't sticking perhaps isn't one worth sticking to.

PREPARE 100 AND DELIVER 3

Just because you can doesn't mean you have to

You are the expert and you have just been booked for the keynote of your career.

Why you? Because you have 25 years' experience in the industry and know more about the topic than anyone else on the planet. Wow, that's great! This could also be a huge problem!

You know so much you could run a nonstop 12-month programme on the topic, but now you have only been given one hour.

Whatever you do, do not give your 25 years of knowledge in one hour as some try to do. You end up completely overwhelming the audience with so much information that nothing really gets through. They end up leaving with no strong messages or with no real value at all.

The decision you have to make when preparing is not what to put in a presentation but what to leave out.

A small handful of relevant takeaways or key messages are so much more powerful than a full smörgåsbord placed in front of your audience where they have no idea where to start.

If you provide good value you will be asked back. You can then share some more. Some speakers use a keynote or a one-hour talk as a tempter to entice people to attend a longer programme or it is followed up by an in-house workshop later in the day.

It doesn't mean you only prepare for your one golden gift though. By preparing more than enough you will be more confident answering questions and you will be open to adjusting your presentation to meet the mood of the audience. This will also demonstrate to the audience that you truly are an expert and you have a wealth of knowledge to share when the time is right.

Many seasoned speakers' advice to new and emerging speakers is "don't go wide, go deep" – meaning, find a topic and keep learning more and more about that topic so you can claim expert status. How can an expert possibly share all their great insights in just one session?

You know the saying "Leave them wanting more". If they don't need you to come back they may buy your book or subscribe to your newsletter to keep the relationship alive and the information flowing.

HAVE A CONVERSATION

Conversation is a two-way street

Remember at school when we were asked to prepare a speech?

I love listening to a well prepared speech, a well thought out argument or an inspirational story.

However, on a commercial level a perfectly crafted speech is the last thing I want delivered to a conference full of employees waiting to be inspired, influenced or informed.

It is far from the perfect delivery method for a training room and it just won't cut it in a workshop. When critiquing my coaching clients who are very stiff, unnatural and struggling with non-verbals, I suggest they stop delivering a speech and start having a conversation.

The immediate transformation is quite incredible.

A conversation can come from the heart, it is not rehearsed word for word, it is natural sounding and the non-verbals are congruent with the message.

When we are having a conversation we are inviting our audience to be involved, to respond and to be immersed in the experience.

A speaker can come across as more authentic when sounding relaxed and comfortable and able to interact more naturally with the audience.

Don't think that you don't have to prepare and rehearse. I always rehearse my opening and closing, I rehearse my signature stories and I even rehearse answering some questions that I feel may be asked during the presentation.

The trick is to make it sound like you are having a conversation. If you make a mistake it is much easier to recover by making comments like "Let me explain that another way" or "Interesting question, my opinion on that is ..." than trying to remember a word-perfect script.

Can you imagine on a longer presentation a keynoter trying to remember a 90-minute script, a trainer trying to remember an 8-hour one or an executive trying to pitch with a speech rather than allowing the board to ask relevant questions and then responding to them accordingly?

I always try to write in a conversational style so my audience feels they are having a chat with me when they are reading my newsletters, blogs or books.

It all helps the audience to get to know the real you.

CRAFT YOUR CREDIBILITY STATEMENT

What gives you the right?

As a presenter your credibility is a critical element of building trust with your audience.

Your audience wants to know why **you** are standing up there speaking to them and why they should be listening to you.

Your credibility statement is a well constructed story about who you are and why you are a resource to them.

Your credibility statement is not always the same, it must be customised and contextualised for each presentation and each audience. For example, if I am presenting to a group of trainers, I will let them know my qualifications and experience as a trainer. However, if I am speaking to a group of women about work/life balance, they are not interested in my training expertise, they are interested that I am a mum of three and I run a busy business.

Your credibility statement is not your CV and it is not a brag statement of why you are so good. It should be crafted in a story-like manner which still gets the message across but also keeps the audience liking you. Use phrases like, "It was my privilege", "I was lucky enough", "When they asked me to ...". Much more humble than I was so good they had to have me.

Why do you have to do this? Pretty simple—because everyone in the audience is wondering about you so let them know as much as you can about who you are. Give enough information to eliminate any doubt that you deserve to be on that platform without taking up precious presentation time. You can't possibly tell them everything in a couple of minutes but you can weave other credibility bites throughout your presentation when sharing a story or an example.

Many times when you are asked to present you have an MC to introduce you. You MUST write your own introduction and send it through to the event organisers. Your introduction is your credibility statement so don't let an MC who doesn't know you tell the audience all about you. The great thing about writing introductions for someone else to read is you can brag a little bit more about your achievements as it is someone else telling the audience about you. Third party endorsements are gold.

Remember when you go through the structure in Principle 11 the first four steps are crucial for setting up your presentation so the audience is ready to learn. Your credibility statement is usually step 2. If you miss out the first four steps you may find yourself having to prove your credibility and theories all the way through the entire presentation and that is hard work.

You do deserve to be there so remove any doubt about the level of your knowledge, skills and experience before you dazzle them with your dynamic presentation.

BE YOUR AUTHENTIC SELF

Being the expert is being you

In this book, the most powerful word for building trust is "authenticity".

An audience wants to know their presenter is telling the truth.

The only way you can build trust and connect with an audience is to be completely yourself.

I hear it time and time again when I present workshops on presentation skills or coach clients: "I want to be able to present like Tony Robbins or Steve Jobs....". My answer is pretty blunt: "Well you can't, you are not them. How about we work on being the best presenter you can be being you."

It is absolutely essential we watch other presenters to learn and grow but we need to ask the questions such as, "Why did that work for them? What can I do that is just as great that can work for me?"

Analyse why the audience responded in a particular way, study the structure they used, admire how they handled questions from the audience then look at how you can integrate great strategies still using your style, your content and your strengths to be just as good. You may even watch some terrible presenters to learn just as much.

So how do you be real, authentic and congruent?

You give a little of yourself in every presentation. You be a real person not just an industry expert. Share some real-life stories, tell them you have also made mistakes, explain your successes, have a laugh and sometimes even show vulnerability.

Be confident to be yourself. What are the strengths you bring to the platform? Are you a little quirky? Do you have something different about you? Showcase these things, be proud of your accent, your culture, your differences. Turn them into your point of difference that makes people talk about you (for all the right reasons).

Even the way you choose to dress when you are presenting tells the audience something about you. Make sure you are consistent with who you are too. Trust is also about reliability. Don't confuse your audience about who you are.

Have you ever wondered why presenters tell so many rags-to-riches stories? "I lost everything and then I got it all back by doing these three easy steps" (not my favourite way to influence, I think I would prefer to learn from someone who didn't lose it all in the first place). But it works because the audience can put themselves in the presenter's shoes and think if they can do it then so can I.

It is just too exhausting trying to be someone you're not, trying to remember which hat to put on. You can't be everyone's favourite speaker but it is much harder to take if they fall in love with the character you are playing and not you.

A presenter who relates and connects will build relationships. Remember, **all business is about relationships**. No-one wants to build a relationship with a person they cannot trust.

From the boardroom to the training room to the conference floor, be honest and be yourself – your audience will love and respect you for it.

19

TRUST IS CURRENCY

Start depositing your platform currency into your business bank account

On the previous page we talked about how being authentic is the only way to honestly build trust. If you use speaking and presenting to build business, trust is now your currency.

Trust builds a relationship, a good relationship builds business, a thriving business builds your bank balance. Trust is currency. Speaking to a group of people is one of the fastest ways to build trust. Many other marketing strategies need at least 10 touch points with a client before a client will trust their views, products or services. A great presentation can do it in just one touch point. But what if you only have an hour to educate, inform, persuade, entertain and build trust? Here are some simple strategies you can use if you need to build trust quickly.

In the first few minutes:

- ✓ Choose your opening statement or action with your key messages in mind
- ✓ State something complimentary about the people, venue, the organisation or the previous speaker (be truthful)
- ✓ Smile
- ✓ Tell them something personal about yourself
- ✓ Ensure you state that your presentation is all about what is in it for them

During the hour:

- ✓ Not too much self-talk
- ✓ Don't waste their time, stick to the point
- ✓ Give lots of value
- ✓ Check in with your audience during the hour. Ensure they are picking up and following the information
- ✓ Always offer some further support in some way after the presentation
- ✓ Maintain eye contact with as many people as you can
- ✓ Be clear of your presentation "Purpose"
- ✓ Have a conversation, not a perfectly rehearsed speech

Always be passionate and committed to your message and, most of all, enjoy every minute of your time on the platform.

Every time you break trust, it's like making a huge currency withdrawal from your account. Do it often enough and you will be broke.

GET CONNECTED

On what level are you connecting?

Have you ever met someone and instantly just clicked with them? And others you may like but you just don't seem to be on the same page as them most of the time. Have you had a friend for many years and now all of a sudden the conversation is just hard work? Maybe the one thing that connected you for all that time isn't there anymore.

We know we must connect with our audience to be able to influence them in any way or inspire them to take action but there are varying ways to do this and there are also different levels of connection.

If you don't understand the level of connection with your audience, you may end up saying comments at the end of the presentation like, "It was a difficult audience today" or "I have no idea why this audience didn't respond as well as last week's".

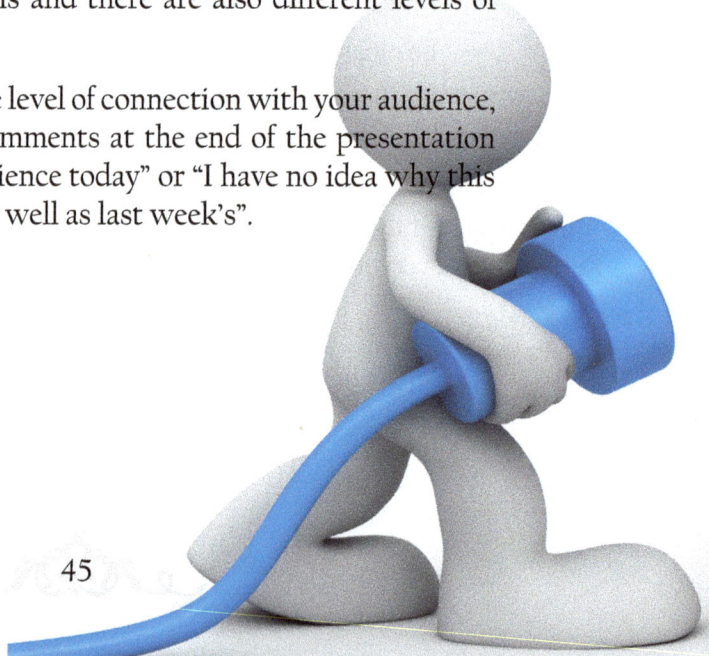

On what level are you connecting?

Intellectually – Is the conversation stimulating? Are you challenging their assumptions?

Spiritually – This does not have to mean religion. Do you make a statement such as, "I think we are all meant to be here today, in this room at this time" and the audience is nodding and agreeing? Or are most of them thinking you are a little loopy? Do they share your belief system?

Emotionally – You are talking from your heart to theirs and they just get it. You may have shared the same experiences and feelings.

Lifestyle – Your lifestyle and lifestyle choices are aligned with theirs. For example, you all own a small business.

Timing – They need your message and help just at this time, they may not mind who the messenger is.

Do your homework with your audience. If most of the audience don't have children, maybe you can miss out a couple of your slides or family stories and replace them with some statistics or facts instead. If you have been chosen to speak to the group because of a personal experience, leave the stats for another day, share more stories and connect heart to heart.

FEAR IS ALL IN THE MIND

It just doesn't feel that way to the truly terrified

Glossophobia is the fear of public speaking, and I have come across my fair share of truly terrified speakers over the years.

Do you have healthy nerves or glossophobia? Many of us just have healthy nerves.

Even the most seasoned professionals get nervous before a big presentation. It is not going to stop them from taking the platform though. Public speaking nerves are a big problem if they are stopping you from achieving your goals.

So what do most people fear? Let's see if we can eliminate some of the stress.

What if I go blank? Have your notes somewhere nearby, pre-write flip charts, take the focus off you for a moment by asking the audience to do something so you can get back on track, and don't panic if you lose your way.

What if I can't answer a question? Ask the audience, say you will cover this later in the session or be honest and say you really don't know the answer but it is a great question.

What if they don't like it? What if they do? Try to look at your information as a gift – sometimes people are thrilled with it and other times people don't love it but are grateful for the intention. It is almost impossible to please everyone but it doesn't stop us trying.

What if they doubt me? If your credibility statement is delivered and you have put steps 1-4 in place at the beginning of the presentation and you are truly committed to your topic, it is highly unlikely this will happen.

What if they challenge me? You can't control what people say but you can control how you respond to them. Keep your emotions in control, pause and respond carefully and appropriately from a place of knowledge and expertise not from a place of defence.

After 26 years of presenting I have yet to meet anyone who woke up in the morning and said to themselves "I am going to ruin Paula's presentation today". No-one really thinks too much about you at all. They are thinking of themselves and what they will get out of the presentation.

If you make it all about you, you will start to feel nervous. Your mindset needs to move to "Today is all about them, every presentation you do is all about them".

Nerves are fear. Try to figure out specifically everything you are fearful of and do something to help remove or reduce the likelihood of it happening.

Do: Think positively about the presentation, prepare well, rehearse, chat to the audience before if you get the chance, get there early and stand in position to gauge how it feels, have some activities up your sleeve if you need to take the focus off you, get there early enough to change or accept anything that doesn't meet your expectations, drink lots of water, get a good night's sleep prior to the presentation, be open to constructive feedback.

Don't: Think negatively about the experience, drink alcohol before the presentation, try to wing it, go in audience blind, arrive with no time to get your mind in the zone, or over-rehearse – and don't be your worst critic.

Everyone makes mistakes from time to time, speaking and presenting is no different. If you have a bad presentation, it's just like a bad day at work. Tomorrow will be better.

You may have heard the saying, "A speaker always has three presentations: the one they planned, the one they gave and the one they wish they would have given." We always hope to hit that mark every time, and most times if you prepare enough you can. The audience rarely notices if we miss a story or a piece of information. They don't know what you have prepared.

The more you do it the more comfortable you will be. You could even be transformed from a truly terrified resister to a confident speaking enthusiast.

Celebrate every time you present because your message and your presentation may have changed somebody's life.

THERE ARE USUALLY NO NAKED PEOPLE IN YOUR AUDIENCE

Visualise yourself being a speaking superstar

The previous principle was about overcoming fear. We are not going to dwell on it though, we are only going to imagine we are speaking superstars.

As silly as that sounds, visualisation is a powerful strategy for removing those limiting beliefs and moving closer to your goals.

I remember when I was studying theatre my teacher told the class if we got nervous to imagine the whole audience naked or in their underwear. I am not quite sure if this was to give us a good laugh or to transfer the power and confidence to the only fully clothed person in the room.

I have always used visualisation to get me in my presenting zone and I know a lot of my speaker colleagues do the same. Where possible I arrange a visit to the venue to view the room or the stage I will be presenting on. This gives me a feel for the room, the size, where everyone will be seated etc. If I haven't been able to do this prior, on the day of the presentation I try to sneak into the room. I stand on the stage, walk around, get a sense of the space I have to work with and I visualise the audience (not naked though). I then know what to expect when I finally do get to take the platform and I always imagine myself giving a stellar performance.

In my previous book *Speaking in the Shower (Presentation Skills Exposed)* I talk about the power of self-talk and how destructive it can be just before a presentation. Are you visualising the audience as hungry animals waiting to pounce or a happy smiling group of individuals ready to receive you with welcoming arms?

Do you visualise yourself shaking hands with audience members after the presentation or having photos with your raving fans?

If you visualise yourself being a nervous, hesitant presenter waiting to crash and burn I am sure that person will always show up. If you want a confident, happy, self-assured leader to show up make sure your mind is seeing and feeling that person. Visualise the speaking superstar.

What can you see now?

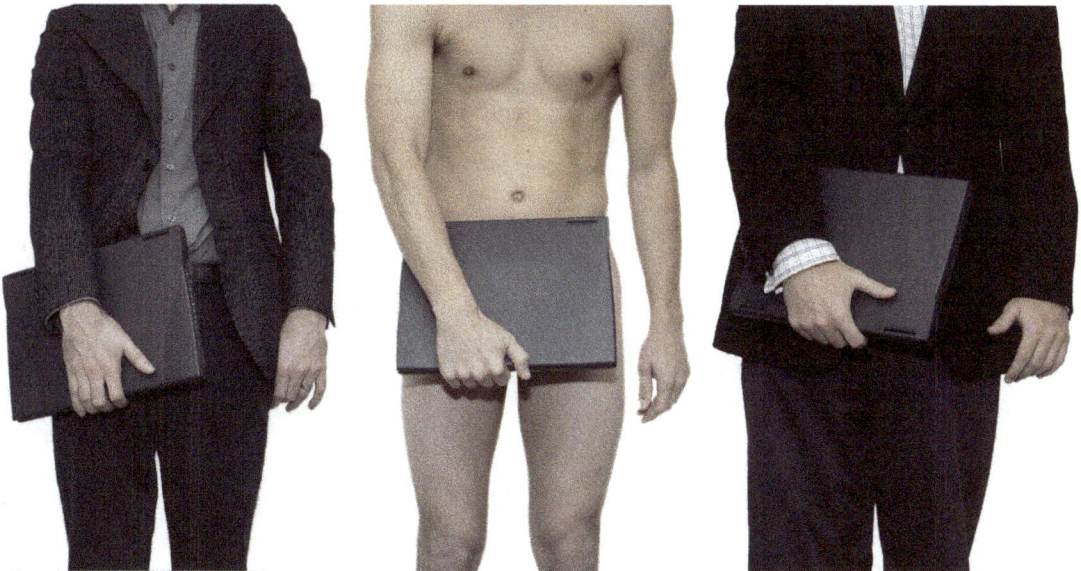

DISCOVER THE POWER
OF INFLUENCE

How to change the minds and hearts of your audience

Every presentation has an element of influence.

As presenters we need to be able to change the minds and hearts of our audiences so they will change behaviours so they can improve their life and the lives of others.

It is human nature for many of us to resist change. If you do not learn the science and practice of influence how can you prepare to change the views and actions of your audience?

How can you pitch a sale in a boardroom or get your message across in a debate?

One of the most successful books on influence ever written is Influence: *The Psychology of Persuasion* by Robert B Cialdini. Research has uncovered six key principles for influence, and these six principles or rules can be easily embedded into the design and delivery of an influential presentation.

1. **Reciprocity**: People tend to return a favour. If you do something for your clients they are much more likely to do something for you. In a presentation it can be as simple as offering a question and answer session so all of their questions will be answered, or allowing more time for an activity. When you ask for more time, you will be amazed at how willing they will be to give you more time.

2. **Commitment and consistency**: Are you demonstrating commitment and consistency with your message or your topic? Commitment and consistency are valued in our society. Are you reminding your audience to be consistent and are you asking them to commit to change?

3. **Social proof**: We all know that if Mrs Jones next door tells us she just used the best vacuum cleaner she had ever used we may be tempted to go out and buy one. An advertisement telling us how good it is would never have this impact. Social proof in a presentation can be a video testimonial of one of your past participants raving about the results he has had from implementing your ideas. Or even statistics from other organisations which dared to change their practices. We all know the power of social media. Same principle.

4. **Authority**: People will tend to obey authority figures, even if they are asked to perform objectionable acts. How will you demonstrate you are an authority on your topic? Your credibility statement will be crafted with this in mind. Your qualifications, your experience, a book you have had published are all pieces of evidence to prove you are an authority on the subject and, of course, because of this you are a trusted resource.

5. **Liking:** People are easily persuaded by other people that they like. Don't underestimate the rule of liking. In sales, research has shown people may choose to buy something from a salesperson they like even if it is more expensive. You must get people to like you in a presentation. This is different to liking all of your ideas. Smile, be authentic and honest throughout and it shouldn't be too difficult. Many presenters' egos are too big for them to get this critical rule. Don't let ego get in the way of people liking you.

6. **Scarcity:** Perceived scarcity will generate demand. For example, saying offers are available for a "limited time only" encourages sales. It is human nature to want what we can't have so the moment you say "I only have three but there are five of you here", people go running because they don't want to be the only person who misses out. Scarcity can be used if you are selling from the platform.

Presenters are sales people, leaders, influencers of change.

If we cannot influence our audience to change we cannot get results.

MAKE THE COMPLEX SIMPLE

Not everyone is going to just get it

Have you ever been at the receiving end of industry jargon and you are not from that industry so have no idea what the person was saying? Or you have been in a conference and the academic presenter is delivering their research in what seems like a foreign language?

World-class presenters have the skill to be able to make even the most complex information simple.

Trainers who know how to break down a skill set into bite-size pieces and allow their participants to practice each step have so much more success than what is considered a "data drop".

When you are designing your presentation it must be aimed at the right level for the audience but this doesn't mean it has to be elaborate and complicated.

Your goal as a presenter is to bring new insights and engage the audience but also make learning and listening to you easy. If you overcomplicate things people will just shut off.

Your presentation must also flow so the audience doesn't get lost. They can follow along, and enjoy a few surprises, but in general they can put the pieces of your presentation jigsaw together to make the whole picture themselves.

The clever use of analogies, metaphors and similes can also help your audience relate to the concept.

An analogy states something is like something else: Life is like a plate of colourful cupcakes. A metaphor suggests something is: Life is a party. A simile suggests something is the same as or like: She was as hungry as a lion; his tummy rumbled like a cement mixer.

Once they hear the analogy, they start connecting the dots and contrasting the elements to your idea or theory.

Pictures really are worth a thousand words (more on this in Principle 33). Pictures will help your audience to see an idea and process it more quickly. You should also use simple models, charts and graphs to demonstrate statistics or steps in a process.

Clever does not mean complicated. Clever is simple. Remember, it is not always the expert on a topic that gets the gig, it's the expert who can get the message across. We sometimes assume our audience has a level of experience or knowledge about the topic or industry so we forget to go through the basics so everyone can catch up or has reference points.

Go through your presentation with a 12-year-old or someone who doesn't understand your industry and see if it makes sense to them. I used to say to my students, "Explain it like I was a 4-year-old". Even though you wouldn't present it at this level it helps you to break down your complex theories into basic easy-to-understand concepts as a starting point.

WE DON'T ALL LEARN
IN THE SAME WAY

Be an educator

According to John Medina in his *Brain Rules*, every brain is wired differently. No two people's brains store the same information in the same way in the same place and we have a great number of ways of being intelligent, many of which don't show up in IQ tests.

Research has also shown we all learn differently too.

You may have heard of Neil Fleming's VARK model. It is one of the most widely used learning preference theories.

Fleming suggests we prefer to learn either by: Visual (learning by seeing), Auditory (learning by hearing), Reading/Writing (learning by reading text, taking notes, research) or Kinaesthetic (hands-on learning).

Honey and Mumford's learning preference research from the 1980s suggests another four types of learner: The Activist (fully immerse themselves in learning activities), the Pragmatist ('get on with things' type people, practical and keen to improve procedures), the Reflector (stand back and ponder, need time to process) and the Theorist (perfectionists, need proof, love systems and models).

This is not to suggest we put any of our participants into boxes; these theories explain there are preferences, but we all enjoy a mix of many methods during a presentation. There are many other profiling tools currently on the market that we can use to find out a little more about our participants.

Although we can't always ask our participants to complete a profiling questionnaire, it does help you as a presenter to understand there are differences – we do not all think the same and we do not all like information presented to us in the same way.

A great presentation or training course has a mix of methodologies to engage all the participants most of the time. Some activities such as group discussions or graphic facilitation will please every learning preference.

I highly recommend that as a presenter you personally complete one of these profiling tools so you can understand yourself better. If you are a theorist you may be more inclined to present your information from the lectern with too many words on too many slides and not allow for any audience interaction because you may prefer to learn this way. Once you are aware of your learning preference you can stand back and have a look at how you have designed your presentation to ensure it's not going to be delivered around your preferences but will appeal to all.

A speaker is also an educator. You need to learn how to teach, train and embed learning.

ATTENTION, ATTENTION, ATTENTION

Adults don't have very long attention spans

What is the average attention span of an adult in a learning environment? There has been much debate about the time frame but most of the research suggests approximately 10 minutes.

This means that at the 10-minute point most adults will check out or let their mind start to wander. Fine if your presentation is only for 10 minutes but what if you have a 90-minute keynote or an 8-hour training day?

You have to ensure that at least every 10 minutes you change the state of your audience. This could be as simple as asking them a question.

Other ways we can keep the attentional spotlight on our presentation are:

- Show a visual.
- Ask them to discuss something with the person next to them.
- Tell a story (emotional arousal helps us to pay attention).
- Give an activity.
- Get them moving.
- Show a video.
- Move around the stage or the room.
- Give them something to touch.
- Play music.
- Ask more questions.
- Get them to write.
- Use voice inflections.

In John Medina's *Brain Rules* he states that "We don't pay attention to boring things" – just because it interests you doesn't mean it is going to excite everyone in the room. He goes on to explain that our attentional spotlight can only focus on one thing at a time. No multi-tasking. The latest neuroscience research also supports this theory, so during your presentation don't have too much going on. One great piece of information which hits home and is put into action is better than 20 pieces going in one ear and out the other.

In your opening your goal is to get attention, you now have to keep the attention until your powerful close.

THE 3 Rs OF PRESENTING: REMEMBER

Remember, Realise and Return on Investment

When you are booked to present, the organisation that pays the cheque will want one big R from the presentation. Their big R is Results. To get results from your presentation you need to be mindful of the three Rs of the information funnel.

Remember – How do I get the audience to remember the presentation?

Realise – How do I get the audience to realise that this information can have a positive impact on their life or their business?

ROI (Return on investment) – How will I measure the effectiveness of my presentation?

Principles 27, 28 and 29 cover each of these Rs.

The first R is about getting your audience to remember as much of the presentation as they can. When designing your presentation keep in mind how much the brain can remember in any given session.

Many presenters do the big data drop, and give so much information the audience is overwhelmed and leaves the presentation remembering not very much at all.

In presenting it really is about quality not quantity. Give enough of the right information in a way in which everyone can remember it.

You can achieve amazing results by the clever use of: tricolon, anaphora, epistrophe, alliteration, simile, analogy, metaphor, acronym, and primacy and recency.

Of course, remembering information doesn't always mean attendees will put it into action so this is why remembering is only one of the Rs of presenting. All three must be embedded into the design of every presentation.

Let's look a little more closely at some of the strategies I have suggested, with some examples.

Tricolon – Also referred to as the rule of three. We tend to remember information in sets of three. (Refer back to Principle 14 – Key messages that stick)

Anaphora – This is the repetition of a word or phrase at the start of several sentences in a row. It is used a lot in political and motivational speeches but can be used in any presentation to help messages stick. I will see, I will hear, I will feel.

Epistrophe – Like anaphora except the repetition of a word or phrase is at the end of several sentences in a row. I see the breeze, I hear the breeze, I feel the breeze.

Alliteration – Using the same first letter for several words that are close together. Hot, Humid, Horrible.

Simile – A figure of speech in which two unlike things are compared using 'like' or 'as'. Her eyes twinkled like the stars; or as big as an elephant.

Analogy – Transferring information or meaning from one thing to another. The Earth's layers are like a piece of cake: the icing is the surface, etc.

Metaphor – A figure of speech in which a term or phrase is applied to something which it is not usually applied to in order to suggest they are alike in some way. A world of hurt; or, Your ship has finally come in.

Primacy and recency – The audience tends to remember the first and last things they do or hear. For this reason we must ensure our opening and closing statements are powerful and align to our key messages.

Acronym – If you really need to get your audience to remember four, five or even seven things, use an acronym. An acronym is a word that is formed from the first letters of other words. Acronyms can be fun to put together and you can use them on models, charts and promotional material. For example – Remember your PASSION when presenting:

Preparation

Authentic

Structure

Stories

Inspiration

Original thoughts

Natural

Can you think of a really cool acronym for your topic? Not only is it your own IP but it is one of the most powerful strategies we can use for people to remember a lot of information as the first letter of each word or sentence acts as a memory trigger.

So don't data drop, deliver your content in bite-sized chunks of information using clever figures of speech and techniques.

THE 3 Rs OF PRESENTING: REALISE

The Aha moments

The craft of designing a presentation is more complex than you may first imagine. Many presenters/trainers/speakers design their presentation or training session only on the basis of the 'remembering' strategy.

I can tell you about hundreds of presentations I have attended and can reiterate much of the content. Not a lot of action was had in the moments, days or months following though. The most powerful presentations I have attended are the ones that I leave and can't wait to get back to the office or my life to action what I have just witnessed or heard. The presenter had made me REALISE that this information can and will change my life for the better in some way.

We have already discussed in earlier principles the importance of the emotional link to the content – the WIIFM (what's in it for me). If the audience does not realise what impact this new information can have on their life once actioned your ability to influence them to take action any time soon is hugely diminished.

A truly wasted presentation.

It's the 'Aha' moments a presenter looks for in a crowded auditorium. The nodding, the excitement on people's faces and the 'penny drop' look in their eyes.

How many Aha moments have you consciously and deliberately placed in the relevant places in your presentation?

We get our Aha moments by using examples or 'before and after', client testimonials, visuals of their new reality, figures on charts and even a glimpse of the future if they don't take action. We sometimes have to show them some pain before providing a solution.

If you do this well enough, convincing people to take action will be a much easier process. If you are selling from the platform, you may even get them waving their credit cards at you instead of you trying to pry them from their wallets.

If you don't see any evidence of success with your message to incite the Aha moments you may need to re-think why you are there presenting this content.

Hmmm. Anyone get an Aha moment reading this page?

THE 3 Rs OF PRESENTING: ROI

ROI does not mean Rate on Invoice

The last of the 3 Rs. If you don't measure the effectiveness of your presentation you will never know what is working and what is not. Success can be a fluke and presentation failure can be just one presentation away.

I would never want to hire a presenter who wings it. I want to be convinced that if I am paying for this presentation the presenter, the concepts, the information and the process are going to get me results. I want to be convinced of this during the consultation process. And I want some evaluation strategy in place to provide this evidence after the presentation has concluded.

Now I know what you are thinking right now – feedback forms don't work. I agree to some extent. A poorly designed feedback form – or happy sheets as we call them – are a complete waste of time. But a well constructed feedback form, customised for each presentation or training programme, can give you valuable information. But the success of the evaluation depends on when and how you are asking for the information to be returned.

A happy sheet at the end of the presentation only measures how people are feeling about the programme at that point in time. They cannot possibly tell you about their success in applying the learning.

According to Donald Kirkpatrick's "four levels of evaluation" model we have four areas we should be evaluating.

Level 1 Reaction – What did they like? How do they feel?

Level 2 Learning – What did they learn?

Level 3 Behaviour – What behaviours have changed as a result of the presentation?

Level 4 Results – Are these changed behaviours getting the required results?

Unfortunately, many presenters never evaluate past level 1.

A happy sheet at the end of the presentation cannot give you these levels of information. A generic survey used for every presentation cannot give you the critical and specific feedback you need across a broad range of items being measured.

You may decide that you prefer not to use a written feedback form at all for measuring the effectiveness of a presentation. There are so many other successful methods.

Other evaluation strategies include:

- Anecdotal evidence
- Sales records
- Future attendance
- Workplace reports and performance reviews
- Observation of behaviours
- Employee retention.

Always measure the return on investment in some way from every presentation.

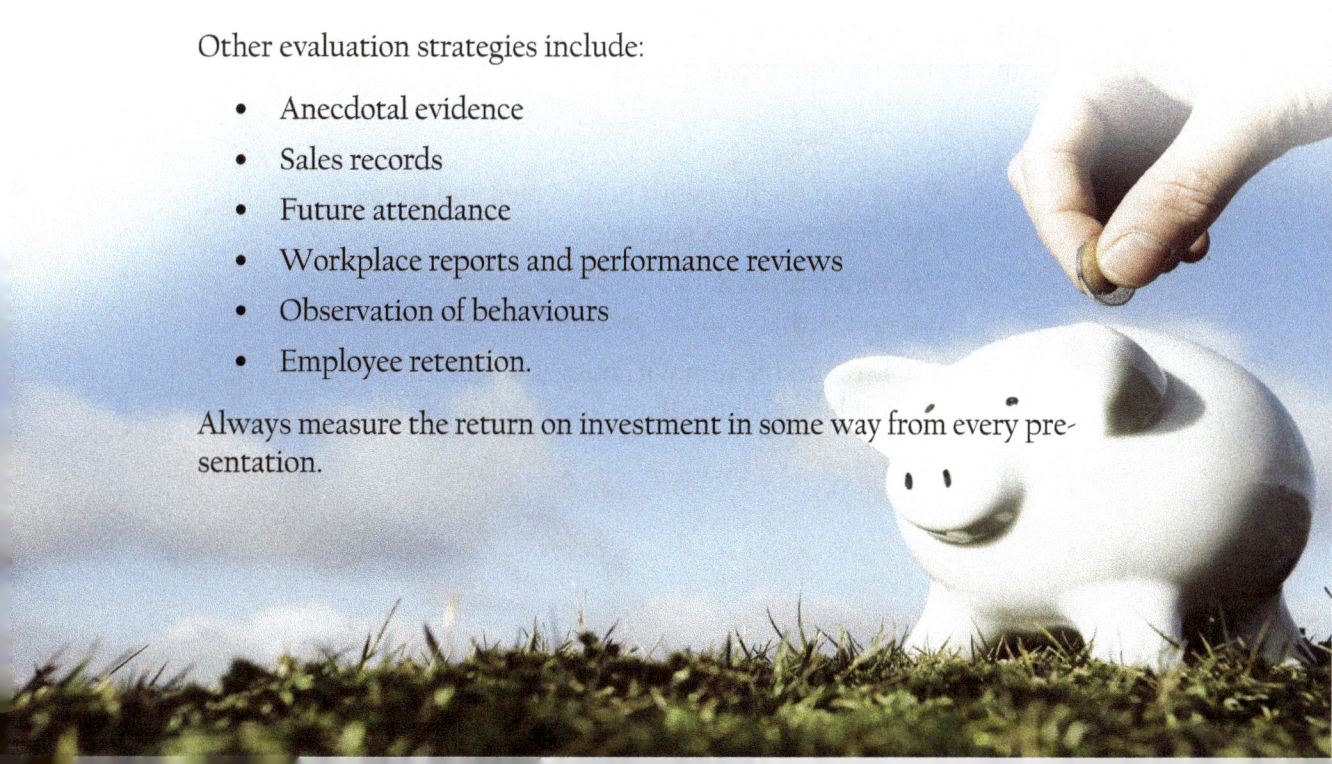

YOUR VOICE IS THE TOOL
OF YOUR TRADE

And your magic wand

Just like any other profession that has their tools of the trade, your most valuable tool as a presenter is your voice.

Learning to use your voice as a powerful tool is critical for engaging and influencing your audience.

A whisper, a pause or a loud outburst can all be as powerful as each other if used in the right way and at the right time.

During presentation skills training we film our participants and review the film in three ways:

- ✓ We watch the film with both screen and sound to review our performance.
- ✓ We watch the film and mute the sound to view our non-verbal communication.
- ✓ We listen to the film without the screen to analyse how effectively we are using our voice.

I recently attended a conference where the presenter was so loud throughout the entire presentation I had to put my hands over my ears. It was meant to be a motivational talk – it felt like I was being preached to. Because of the way the presenter used his voice, I completely turned off and missed whatever the message was meant to be.

One of my favourite presenters is an educator and professional speaker who is a very quietly spoken man and almost uses a whisper. He pauses just before saying something significant and even though he is quiet his inflections are interesting and rich in tone. He is a powerful presenter.

When presenting be mindful of your:

Pace – Not too fast but not sounding as if you are medicated either. A pace that is easy to follow, and that can speed up and slow down when appropriate.

Pitch – If you want to influence and make an important point, drop your pitch at those crucial moments. A deeper sounding tone at the end of a sentence is more authoritative than a higher octave.

Inflection – Modulation of the voice during a presentation delivers a much more engaging presentation. Use lots of expression throughout and ensure you emphasise key messages and phrases.

Pause – The powerful pause. Practice pausing just before an important word or message; it keeps the audience on the edge of their seats. Don't just gloss over important facts, figures or messages; pause before you reveal them.

Volume – The right level for the size of the room and audience. You can also use volume and an inflection to make a serious point or to be excited about some of your content. Being too loud can overwhelm your audience. Being too quiet can annoy your audience.

Protect – You do need to protect and look after your voice. It needs lubricating, it needs practice and it needs rest. If you have a large audience don't be tempted to speak loudly throughout the presentation, request a microphone. If you have a sore throat or it sounds hoarse, don't just push on and try to speak as you can do a lot of damage to your vocal chords. Some damage can be permanent.

Avoid alcohol or caffeine before a presentation. These act as diuretics. This loss of fluids dries out the voice. Alcohol also irritates the mucous membranes that line the throat.

Accents can be an asset or a liability. If you have a strong accent, make sure your participants can understand you. You may have to speak more slowly and ensure you are using your non-verbals to reinforce your message.

Always get feedback on the way you use your voice during your presentation. If you are getting negative feedback you may want to seek the services of a voice coach.

Remember though, your voice is as unique as your fingerprint. Use it to your advantage and to stay authentically you.

YOUR GESTURES MEAN BUSINESS

The power of non-verbal communication

A smile is a universal language.

Thumbs up can mean: "All good" "Spot on".

Or a hand that pushes forward can state: "I've had enough" "Not now" "Stop".

We use powerful non-verbal communication every day and probably without thinking about it. What if you found out that your non-verbal communication skills were stopping you from getting your message across in the boardroom, during a conversation or throughout a high-stakes presentation?

You can influence, educate or inspire through your gestures as well as your speaking. Communication is so much more than just the words we say.

There is science and art to all forms of communication. The art and science of non-verbal communication has also been referred to as body language or non-verbal intelligence.

You can use hand gestures during a presentation to make a strong point or reinforce your message. You can use non-verbal gestures during a presentation to appear friendly and let the audience know you are open for discussion and questions. You can also use your eyes, hands and stage anchors during a presentation to guide your audience through a learning journey.

A stage anchor is when you position yourself at a specific place on the stage in your presentation to share a story, a main point or the time of day. Every time you refer back to this part of the presentation you go and stand at the same place. Every time you now go back to that position, even if it's an hour later, the audience knows you are taking them back to that story, event, message or time of the day without having to verbalise it. It forms part of your presentation choreography.

Even when we are using verbal communication during a conversation or a boardroom meeting we need to integrate strong non-verbals as they make our messages more concrete and believable.

According to Michael Grinder (a world guru in non-verbal communication) we can appear more credible and intelligent by learning and practising the science of non-verbals – a must for every presenter. By following Michael's advice and training over the years I personally learnt so much more about how to make my own presentations more powerful and influential.

Don't underestimate the power of your eye contact either during a presentation. Now, what I am about to say may challenge everything you believe or have been taught about not reading your slides during a presentation.

I say do read many of your slides. If your slides are designed well you won't have to read a page full of bullet points or small text but you can look at your slides if you want the audience to look at them.

Because we have been overtrained in eye contact the audience may not feel comfortable breaking eye contact with you when you are speaking to them.

Even if you hand gesture to a slide when you are still talking to them most of the audience will still be looking at you or they may be confused about where to look. If you turn to look at the slide you are referring to, you will find the audience will follow your eyes and look at the slide too. When you turn away from them and look at the slide, the audience now has permission to break eye contact and look at the slide with you. If you don't want the audience to look at the slide, blank the screen.

This can also work when sharing one of your stories with the audience. If you want them to visualise 'looking out of the window' you look out of the window too. Use your eyes to help the audience to see.

Remember in the last principle I suggested viewing a film of your presentation with the sound muted. This is so you can view it and see if your non-verbals are strong during the main points, that you are not flapping your arms around without any purpose and to see how congruent your body language is with your message.

Non-verbal pauses are just as powerful as verbal pauses too. Hold your gesture until you have finished making the point. This helps reinforce the importance of what you have just said.

Help your audience visualise your message not just listen to it. The more senses you engage the deeper the level of learning.

TAKE A RISK

Out of your comfort zone

Do you know your presentation inside-out and back-to-front without any need to rehearse?

Do you get averagely good scores every time you present?

Have you been doing it the same way for years?

If you have answered 'yes' to any of these you may be a good presenter but wouldn't you like to be an awesome presenter who people are talking about a week, a month or even years after your presentation?

Sometimes, the bigger the risk the greater the presentation. Calculated risk, of course. New and emerging presenters are taking risks every day. They are putting their new skills in to practice, presenting and training by trial and error and just getting a feel for who they are as a presenter and what is working well for them. When we have been presenting for a while we have the tendency to stay within our comfort zone, to have the attitude of "if it's not broken why fix it?"

Even experienced presenters need to learn and grow. Our audiences evolve and their expectations change! If you want to stay at the top of your game you need to evolve too – to get the WOW back into your work, your presentation, your craft. World-class presenters are WOW presenters.

Take the time to go to conferences, watch TED talks online, discover which presenters people are talking about. Don't try to be those presenters but do learn from them. Make that affirmation to be a WOW presenter too.

Some risk-taking suggestions are:

- Involve the audience more
- Play a game
- Be controversial
- Play music
- Change your slide platform
- Reveal more about yourself
- Tell stories
- Deliver an unusual opening
- Use some props
- Present without slides
- Introduce new models
- Bring your authentic self to the platform

Being too comfortable is boring. Bring some energy and spark back into your design and delivery. Is it a little dangerous? Of course. Will there be some setbacks? Probably. Will it be fun? Absolutely. Get those creative juices flowing.

Risk taking is part of growth. I challenge you to strive to reach your full presenter potential.

NO MORE DEATH BY POWERPOINT

Slideshows are sideshows

Let's start by stating that PowerPoint is a software programme. It is not the presentation methodology. The term is a slideshow.

Then understand that as a presenter your slideshow is your sideshow. You and your message are the show. You and your message should always play centre stage.

To use or not to use slideshows during a presentation could possibly be the greatest debate to ever occur between presenters.

When a slideshow is used with skill and designed with expertise to support a presentation it is one of the greatest gifts we have ever been presented with in this industry. When it is used poorly, it is a terrible form of torture we insist on subjecting our audiences to in almost all learning platforms.

So here is my take on slides:

1. If we would like a visual to support our message, we present a slide with an image on it.

2. If we have text on the slide, the words are carefully selected to help reinforce our message.

3. If the person at the back of the room cannot see everything on the slide clearly it is a poorly designed slide.

4. If you want your audience to read, give them a document or a handout.

5. Put a concept on the slide, hand a document with detail to the audience.

6. Always use a remote clicker/presenter throughout your presentation so you can move around the room or stage.

7. Blank out the screen (by using the presenter or pressing B for black or W for white on the keyboard) when you are talking at length or answering questions.

8. Don't jump slides; enter the slide number and press enter if you have to go a long way back or forward.

9. Embed movie clips rather than ending the slideshow and then resuming it after the clip.

10. Simplicity is powerful.

11. You should never start planning a presentation by opening your slideshow software.

12. Your slideshow is not your crutch and it is not there to keep you on track. It is there to provide visual support for your content and message.

13. If your technology failed, you could still deliver a knockout presentation.

14. Your slideshow should be useless without you presenting it.

15. Revisit Principle 31 about reading or not reading your slides

16. Must read *Presentation Zen* by Garr Reynolds.

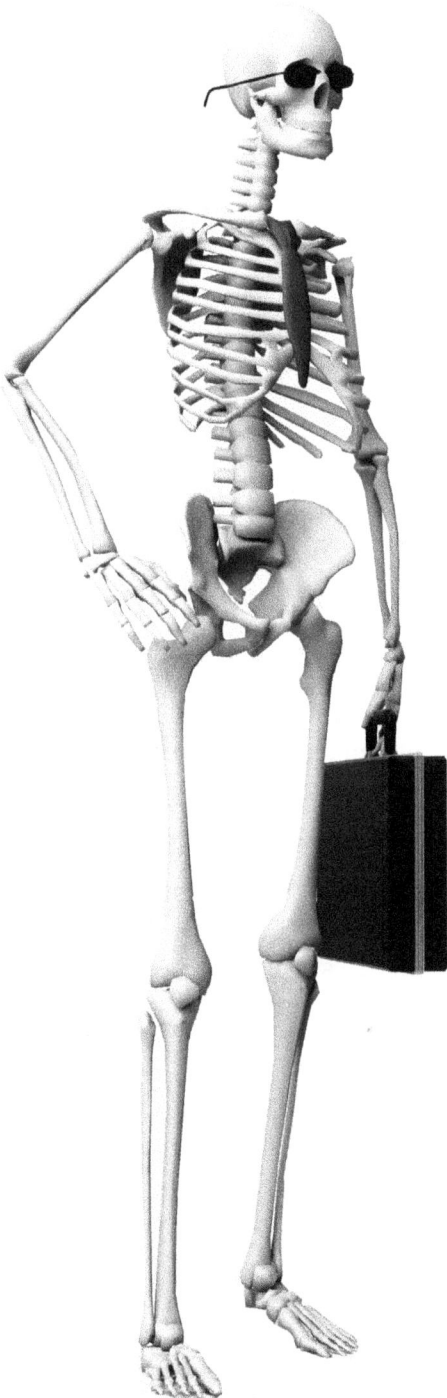

If it's that simple, why are we constantly subjected to death by PowerPoint? Because we have lazy presenters, inexperienced trainers or ridiculous workplace policies that include PowerPoint purgatory.

Have you ever been at the receiving end of the "Here is our organisational template for PowerPoint"? The template with the company logo on every slide, room for 15 lines of text per slide and a pack of 100 slides for each 30-minute presentation. Then they complain about the boring presentations.

Ever noticed where the screen is at a rock concert? Correct, it is to the side of the stage. The rock star is centre stage. You and your content must be the rock star of the presentation. Not your software package.

Slides are a gift, a gift to help you elevate your status to 'Celebrity Speaker' not 'Infamous Bore'.

VISION DOMINATES ALL OTHER SENSES

What are they looking at?

Following on from slideshows, why do we use slideshows at all? Because there are more visual learners in our audiences than any other type of learner. In fact, vision is our dominant sense, it takes up at least half of our brain's resources.

According to John Medina in his *Brain Rules* research, "We learn and remember best through pictures, not through written or spoken words. We are incredible at remembering pictures. Hear a piece of information, and three days later you'll remember only 10% of it. Add a picture and you'll remember 65%."

He goes on to discuss tests performed years ago that showed that people could remember hundreds of photographs with 90% accuracy several days post-exposure, even though subjects saw each picture for about 10 seconds. Accuracy rates a year later still hovered around 63%.

How would you like 63% of your presentation to be remembered after a year?

Yes, another reason why you need to redesign your slideshows to include more images than text.

Your slides are not the only way to provide visual stimuli to help your participants to learn. Writing or drawing key points on flip charts and whiteboards can provide the same visual anchors. Playing a game of charades, giving a demonstration or using props are also just as powerful.

An activity I use often in my classroom to summarise is an artwork exercise. It is an extremely simple activity yet so effective. I instruct small groups to summarise the day's learnings on butcher's paper using a set of coloured markers. The only rule is there can be no words on their page only pictures or symbols. They then present their visual masterpiece to the class. Not surprising at all that the group remembers that piece of artwork, and their classmates' work, long after the programme has concluded, therefore remembering the content of the programme.

Your challenge as a presenter is to engage as many senses as you can but if vision is the dominant sense your presentation must be structured in a way to help your audience see your message.

Presentation methods such as storytelling or short video clips work really well if the message is rich in emotion and visually stimulating. They embed in the memory much better than facts and figures delivered in a sea of bullet points.

When you are presenting, your non-verbal communication skills are just as critical to getting your message across more effectively because you are now adding the visual effects to support your words.

So what visual aids are in your tool box? What can you bring into your presentations to help your audience to see?

How visually stimulating are your presentations? How visually stimulating are you?

TECHNOLOGY IS YOUR FRIEND

I wish I could keep the same friends for life though

Do you ever feel overwhelmed with the amount of technology or the number of online applications that are available for us today? I know I do.

Twenty years ago, our presentation technology was an overhead projector and the occasional video (which we showed on a TV screen).

The presentation technology that is available to us today is amazing. We can present to a live audience without leaving our office. We can conduct live polls in a conference and display the instant results. We can automate our business to send out learning programmes in sequence at specific times. And I am sure by the time this book has been on the shelf for a year or two there will be another 20 options to consider.

Technology can be our friend during a presentation but it can also be a distraction. You need to ask yourself the question: What is the most effective way for this audience to get my message? Sometimes good old butcher's paper and a conversation is the best way, other times bringing in the cameras, the microphones and the latest gadgets for all to play with is the best way.

If you do choose to use technology during a presentation ensure you know how to use it or have adequate support people present. Your paying audience should not be subjected to trials, sound checks, flat batteries, inadequate connectability or incompetence in the application of the media.

The latest applications and technology can also take your business and presentations to a much wider audience. A global audience. One recording of your presentation can produce a product – a presentation product that can be viewed any place and at any time by anyone.

Outdated technology or lack of current technologies during your presentation may damage your credibility as a presenter. Remember though, only use it when it is needed to either enhance the learning experience of the participants, to reach a wider audience or to help get your message across. Cost savings alone is usually not the right reason to be introducing new technologies in presenting.

Don't rely on technology to work. You must still be the superstar presenter that can always present a dynamic and engaging presentation with nothing but yourself and a great message.

DESIGN AND REHEARSE YOUR CHOREOGRAPHY

Move with purpose

Yes, you must choreograph your presentation. Stagecraft is an essential presentation skill to be learnt and mastered.

Do not choreograph every step of a three-hour workshop – that would be unnatural. You must always look natural when you are on the move. Move naturally but always move with purpose.

During your design phase include where you will be standing to deliver key points. When using stage anchors (as discussed in Principle 31) decide where the best place for these anchors will be.

Undoubtedly the most powerful place in the room is front centre stage. I always try to deliver my openings, critical key messages, calls to action and my closing from this point. The rule of 'less is more' for key points can be used here: the less movement, the more powerful the message sounds. Standing still, in one place, with minimal hand gestures, gets that point across with no distraction.

When you do move ensure it is not because you are nervous or bored. If you want to connect with the audience or ask a question you may want to move forward and lean towards them. Or move to one side of the stage to a specific group or individual in the audience to refer to them. I may even walk in silence to the middle of the room as if I am thinking, then stop to deliver a story or a key piece of information.

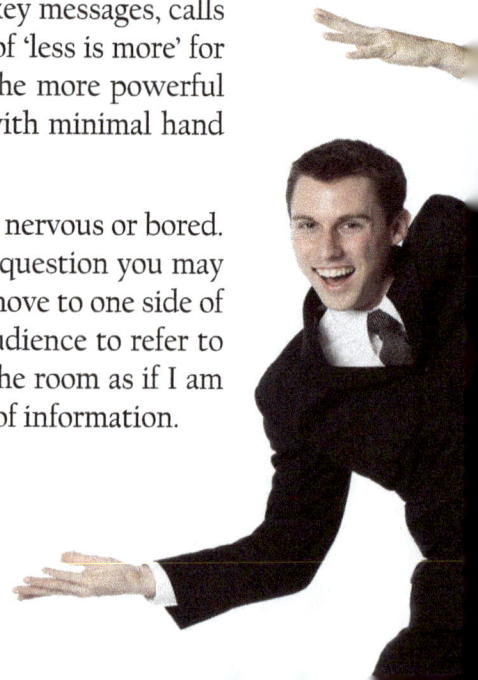

Many presenters let their nerves get the better of them and start to pace, fidget or stand there tapping their foot. This unnecessary movement detracts from the presentation and the message. Filming yourself is vital for reflection. Are you moving too much or too little? Do you fidget or stand in a position that does not command authority like the fig-leaf position (hand in front of crutch) or legs crossed? A good strong position is what we call a 'neutral stance'. Feet apart, toes slightly facing outward and hands in front ready for your first strong hand gesture.

If you are presenting from a lectern (although I suggest you do everything to ensure you are not stuck there) do not lean or hang on to it. Stand and use your hand gestures as if you did not have the barrier there in front of you.

Remember, you can be just as engaging by using your body as your voice. You can squat down to whisper, stand tall on your tippy toes or dance when the music is playing.

If you have to work with a microphone, ditch the hand-held and work with a lapel or a headset to ensure you are free to move. I prefer a headset as the microphone moves with your head so the volume stays consistent. Sometimes with a lapel microphone the volume disappears when you turn your head and makes your words sound a little distorted. Unless you are experienced with a hand-held microphone you may accidentally move the microphone too close or too far away from your mouth during the presentation and imagine how difficult it would be to use your hand gestures with a remote presenter in one hand and a microphone in the other.

If you are presenting with slides ensure you move away from the screen if you want the audience to focus on the screen and move back to centre stage and blank the screen for important discussions. Be careful not to walk or stand in front of any low-lying data projectors as well.

The last point to state is you MUST rehearse. Your choreography is just as important as the words of your presentation. Remember, presenting is science and art.

Stagecraft is both.

MANAGE THE ENERGY IN THE ROOM

Take control

Have you ever walked into a room and felt the energy. It may have felt like a warm and friendly place to be or you could cut the air with a knife.

Training rooms and conference floors are no different. You may not even be responsible for the state of the energy when you take the platform. The last speaker could have left them feeling flat, half of their staff could have just been laid off, or it could be as simple as it's just after lunch.

This is why a great MC is worth every penny. An experienced MC will manage the energy of the room by pulling out icebreakers, getting the audience to interact more or by bringing forward a break if possible before the next speaker is announced.

However, if you are taking the floor and during the presentation you notice the audience is non-responsive, argumentative or people are leaving the room you need to take control.

Keeping to your structure and framing your presentation well at the beginning can minimise many unexpected disruptions from the audience; however, it may not eliminate them altogether. You can't control what someone will say or do; you can control how you react to it.

Sometimes the smaller the audience the more difficult it is to manage, as the clown, the know-it-all, the challenger, or the 'don't want to be there' people take it upon themselves to be a spokesperson or they are easier to spot in the room causing a distraction for the presenter.

Synergy! Use synergy to energise your room. (Synergy is the interaction of elements that when combined produce a total effect that is greater than the sum of the individual elements.) Encourage the positive energy in the room to be contagious. By activating and managing the positive interaction between audience members effectively you can lift the energy in the room immediately. Well chosen activities or questions you introduce can help you in this quest.

For example, "Tell the person next to you and the person behind you the best thing that has happened to you this year", or "give each other a high five for every question you get right".

You are always going to get the clown or the know-it-all in the audience; accept that but don't view it as a negative. Value the diversity and what they can bring to your presentation rather than spending all your energy trying to quieten them.

You have heard the expression "there is no such thing as a bad audience, only bad presenters"! I don't exactly agree with that statement but it certainly has some merit.

It is your presentation so take full responsibility for it. Get there early to change seating arrangements if you need to, bring in some props for the participants, let the audience know what to expect prior, find out who your audience are, acknowledge the elephant in the room or bring some much needed humour to the presentation.

You can't complain after the presentation that it didn't work well because you got the after-lunch time slot; you knew you were presenting after lunch when energy may be low so plan for it.

However sometimes, whatever icebreaker we pull out of our presenter toolbox or whatever audience sing-song we request just doesn't work. Every audience responds differently, so learn to adapt your presentation and your activities to match the audience at that time. Have in your toolbox many "how to " strategies for managing audience energy and behaviour.

Examples of these may be:

- ✓ Being open to adapting your presentation
- ✓ Assessing the energy of the room before introducing activities
- ✓ Framing the presentation correctly
- ✓ Acknowledging people's feelings
- ✓ Setting boundaries and expectations
- ✓ Allowing time for questions
- ✓ Respecting the audience and the current situation

If your audience trusts and respects you they will be more inclined to follow your lead and join you in a positive and productive presentation journey.

A great presenter doesn't just manage an audience, they lead an audience.

TELL ME A STORY

Stories help us to learn

A good story is engaging, a great story is inspirational, a relevant story well told can be life changing.

Once upon a time there was an aspiring presenter. A red-headed chap who stood out with his curly locks, crooked teeth and wide vivacious smile. He was definitely not the best looking young man in the village but there was an authentic charm about him that made people relate and connect with him instantly. The week before his first ever keynote presentation he stopped at the village bookstore to purchase a book. A newly published book that came highly recommended by his trusted and well respected presentation skills coach. He was so nervous about his presentation he was contemplating cancelling it, but he knew if he did this he could risk his credibility and everything he had worked so hard to achieve in the organisation.

He decided to hold off one more day until he read the book. He read every page, every principle and every word of this inspirational and fabulous book on the very first day as he just could not put it down. Everything he ever wanted to know about presenting was right in front of his eyes. Over the next week he rehearsed his presentation using the principles he learnt throughout the pages of *Powerful Presentation Principles*. The night before the presentation he drifted off to sleep feeling much more confident and relaxed about the day that awaited him than he had ever felt before. That night he dreamt he was a confident, charismatic presenter who received a standing ovation from the audience.

He applied the lessons of *Powerful Presentation Principles* that very next day and was branded a speaking superstar and got his standing ovation. In fact, he presented a copy of his favourite book to all attendees so they too could always be confident, powerful presenters.

The End

Okay, I've had my fun now but there is a point here. Let's see if you can remember.

What colour was his hair? Where did he get the book? Who told him to get it? How long did it take him to finish the book? What did he dream about? Why didn't he cancel the presentation? What was the gift he gave to the audience and why?

Stories anchor in the brain in a different way. Stories evoke emotion. Stories can engage the audience in a way no other presentation methodology can.

Presenters who use stories during their presentation may be known for their signature story or they may have a catalogue of stories to choose from that they can re-purpose for specific target groups.

When choosing a story to share, ensure that it:

- ✓ Is relevant to this audience
- ✓ Has a learning point
- ✓ Is not too long
- ✓ Has characters that can come alive
- ✓ Is in a sequence that the audience can follow easily
- ✓ Has a touch of mystery
- ✓ Has a few Aha moments
- ✓ Uses emotion to cause the audience to take action

In an interview for National Speakers Association Robert McKee (legendary screenwriter) confirmed just how much speakers can learn from Hollywood. Robert states the audience wants a story because a story fits with the mind. It is how the mind absorbs, sorts and structures reality.

He goes on to talk about the structure of a story. "Start the story by establishing your world and showing life in balance, then throw it radically off balance with an event that rouses and restores balance."

Stories can be used to immerse listeners in your products, your services and your brand. A well told story can influence and engage, and even though your C Suite clients still insist on facts and figures as well it doesn't mean the whole presentation has to be structured that way.

For thousands of years, our ancestors always used the power of story to teach their young. It is how wisdom (and some myth) was passed down through the generations. So why did we stop? Do we think we are too sophisticated to share stories in modern business? I hope not. Stories are very sophisticated. They can make the complex seem simple, the very strange seem relevant and the results seem achievable.

Always rehearse your stories. This ensures you are comfortable with the flow, the time frame, the animation needed and how to use your voice for the greatest impact.

Stories really do anchor in the brain in a different way. If you design and tell your story well your participants will be able to remember the elements of the story, the characters, where the events took place, the emotion they felt and the sequence of events. They will also recall the moral of the story and the learning point with more impact than a bunch of facts and figures.

If you have ever played the memory game where a list is presented to you for 30 seconds and then after a period of time you need to recall what was on the list you may have only been able to remember up to half a dozen items. A memory strategy is to make up a story around the items on the list; you then recall the story in sequence allowing you to recall many more or all of the items. Give it a try.

Revisit Principle 34 about visual memory: "Hear a piece of information, and three days later you'll remember only 10% of it. Add a picture and you'll remember 65%." Try to provide images and visual stimuli throughout your storytelling. It increases memory exponentially.

Your stories can also build trust and a connection with your audience as you are sharing a little more about yourself. No-one will question your credibility if you can demonstrate you have a lot of personal experience around the topic you are presenting.

We all have stories and experiences to share. Don't think you need a rags-to-riches tale or a devastating event to have a story worth listening to – the people and events around you every day could fill 1,000 presentations. It is just choosing the right one, at the right time, for the right message, for the right audience.

Make your stories a part of how you and your presentations are remembered. Make your stories an integral part of who you are and what your speaking brand represents.

ADULTS LIKE TO PLAY TOO

Games and puzzles are not just for the kids

In a consultation prior to a leadership programme I was delivering, the conservation went like this:

> **Client:** "They're all guys, they're not going to want to play those silly games that some trainers play. Can we just stick to the facts and the content?"

> **Paula:** "I hear what you are saying. I promise you I will not make the guys do or participate in anything that is not relevant."

> **Client:** "Yeah, okay, but I am a bit nervous about it. They're just not that type."

Did I introduce games, activities and puzzles to the four-day programme? Of course. Not all day every day but strategically placed throughout the programme when active learning was needed.

Evaluation from attendees:

Favourite part of the programme "The toothpick game, wow that was powerful, I had no idea that I reacted to instructions like that." And another: "That activity we did with creative thinking, people really do think that differently, I had no idea."

Just like storytelling, games and puzzles as a training or presentation methodology can be a powerful way to get a message across in an interactive and engaging way.

When planning your training or presentation, you are asking yourself: "How do I get my message across? What is an engaging way to bring this message to the audience so they will remember it, realise it and take action so they can achieve results?"

Games and puzzles can do this.

Here are some topics and some presentation methods to match. Which ones would you choose?

Teaching someone to organise a learning environment

1. Draw them on a flip chart

2. Present a slide and describe it, or

3. Give them a Lego board and a box of Lego with a key to what each piece of Lego represents and ask them to build an appropriate leaning environment for an ABC lesson and then share with the group why they have done it this way. (Eyes light up when big people get to play Lego.)

Summarise the day's learning.

1. Ask questions

2. Give a test, or

3. Give a crossword puzzle with a prize for the winning couple. (Free online tools can put a crossword together for you using your information within seconds.)

Leadership characteristics

1. Present a slideshow

2. Have a discussion, or

3. Give a chunk of Blu-tack and a bowl of toothpicks to a team of five and ask each team to build the highest tower in one minute without any questions or instructions. Then ask an observer group who are not in the building team to report on a list of questions about the leadership behaviour of each team member. (Fish bowl method.)

Valuing diversity

1. Give out a workbook to complete on the topic
2. Present a video, or
3. Put them in the outback for a week, or use roleplays with actors.

There are many more examples, and books have been written about the games and puzzles you can play in training rooms and conferences. Start collecting a full set of props, activity ideas and games you can keep in your presenter toolkit that you can bring out at the right time to really get the fun and the wow back into your presentations.

Learning should be fun. When people are having fun, they are much more relaxed. When people are relaxed they are more open to new experiences and new learning.

Games are big business in the corporate world. There are corporate theatre groups, video gaming specialists and even live events where the entire audience play characters in a corporate stage show.

Learners like to be actively engaged in learning so go and have some fun.

Adults like to play when they are given permission to do so, so give them permission – you will be amazed at how much fun you and 1,000 suits can have in one big room.

HONOUR THY SOURCE

You don't always have to bring fresh content

It's okay to borrow someone else's content. It is not okay to steal it.

So what is the difference? You honour thy source on every occasion and tell the audience where it came from.

Many times we can't bring fresh content to the platform and that's okay – we may be presenting the latest research on a topic and didn't do the research, or we may love a quotation from a book we recently read that clearly aligns with our message.

Don't ever present information and pass it off as if it were yours. It is just dishonest. The real author or thought leader should always be recognised. It could have been the result of years of hard work for this person and what gives you the right to pretend it's yours? If you don't know who said it or whose work it is, state "author unknown" but let people know where you found the information. You may be surprised that someone in the audience can help you out with the author.

Another reason is, just like any other lie, you will probably be found out. Trust is everything in business. You break trust and your credibility and integrity will be in question.

If I ever find out that someone is using my content without permission or recognition I would choose never to do business with that person.

Be aware of current copyright laws and any other legislation that affects the use of other people's material in your presentations too. You don't want to end up with a law suit against you.

Just because you can access it for free does not mean you can use it for commercial gain. Many products state you can only use it for personal use unless you have permission or pay for the rights to use in a commercial space.

If you do want to use other people's material it is very easy to drop them a line asking for permission or at least to let them know of your intentions if it is something you have the right to use. They may even be very flattered and give you more interesting resources they have developed for you to use.

It is okay, of course, to go to professional development programmes or read books to get great ideas to use in your presentations – that's what those events and books are there for. Just be careful about the line you are crossing when delivering the ideas to your audience. Did you just learn a concept and are now aligning it with your own IP or are you just pinching a great idea and giving everyone the impression it is your very own original idea?

If you are at a multi-speaker event and the speaker before you used some content you were going to present, honour thy source and also acknowledge the previous speaker if you still choose to present the content. Use phrases like, "John stated the ABC of Leadership in the last presentation. I also love this model and I would like to add..." Acknowledging sources and other speakers will also get the audience on your side and, in turn, will build trust.

The easiest and safest way is to always honour thy source in every presentation when it's not your original work you are presenting. If in any doubt, don't use it.

KEEP TO TIME

Be on time, stay on time and leave on time

This principle shouldn't really need any further explanation. Isn't this just about manners and courtesy and behaving in a professional manner? You know the things your mum or dad taught you. If only business people applied those simple lessons in life to business how easy it would be for everyone.

I have lost count of how often platform professionals abuse the time they have been allocated by event managers.

It doesn't occur to them that their lack of respect for time management can inject a whole spectrum of problems into the successful management of an event.

Be on time: Don't ever, ever be late for a presentation. What does late mean? Too late to be completely organised and in the right state to take the platform when your time is announced. Your reliability and time management is a reflection of how professional you are. Being on time shows respect for the organisers, the stage crew and your audience. It doesn't matter how busy you are or how important you perceive yourself to be. Your time is not more important than anyone else's (a strong lesson from my mum).

I recently attended a multi-speaker event where the special guest speaker was a very high-profile businessman. The car he was in with his business managers was stuck in traffic in the middle of the city on the way to the presentation. The event manager was feeling a bit nervous at the prospect of no speaker and thousands in the audience, so he phoned to find out where they were. This very high-profile businessman jumped out of the car in the pouring rain and ran down Perth's main business district street unaccompanied to ensure he arrived on time. He demonstrated that it doesn't matter who you are; he made a commitment to someone to be on time and on time he was. Just a little wet and puffed.

Stay on time: As a presenter it is your job to manage your time during your presentation. This is why rehearsing your presentation is vital. You can't always time your presentation to the last second as you don't know what questions will arise from the audience or whether you will have to repeat a concept, but you can keep an eye on the time to ensure you give enough attention to every important key message or concept you intended to present. My remote presenter has a timer on it and I can set it to vibrate in my hand when I have 5 or 10 minutes to go, or you can ask someone to be your timekeeper and give you a wave at the half-time mark and when you have 5 minutes left. If you don't manage your time you may find yourself done and dusted before you are meant to be leaving the stage or rushing to fit in your crucial powerful closing.

Leave on time: You have been asked to present for a specific amount of time, not 10 minutes either side of this. If you think you will finish early invite a few more questions, pose a question to the audience or give the audience a quick activity to participate in but don't finish early. At the other end, it doesn't matter how much the audience seems to love you – finish and leave on time.

You can always open up the discussion at another time or tell the audience they can speak to you in the break, but your official presentation should finish on time. If you take another 10 minutes at a multi-speaker event you have just stolen 10 minutes from the next speaker or made it very messy for the catering staff waiting on the sidelines to serve a now cold meal.

There is a time schedule for a reason. Be professional and stick to it.

Your time management is not only at the event but it may extend to before or after the event. Have you got your presentation promotional material on time so the flyers can be printed? Have you forwarded any hand-outs by the due date to be printed? Did you need to order any resources to arrive on time? If you promised to send out some additional material after the event, keep your promise and deliver in a timely manner.

Time to thank Mum for all the lessons learnt, and remember to pass them down to your own kids when it's time for them to become speaking superstars (or just very nice people).

In the speaking industry there are superstars and there are prima donnas just like in any other industry.

Be the professional presenter people talk about for all the right reasons. When the organiser states: "It was a pleasure doing business with you", you can be confident it is sincere and not sarcasm.

There is no room for arrogance if you want to be asked back. Unless you really are a speaking rock star who people will book regardless of your attitude just be easy to deal with.

BE EASY TO DO BUSINESS WITH

Back to the lessons Mum taught you

Don't choose who to be nice to either, that's another form of arrogance. Be helpful and courteous to everyone in the team and everyone in the audience. This includes the AV guys, the caterers, the stage crew, the ticket salespeople, the admin staff, the MC, the other speakers, the marketing people, the cleaning team, and all who have come to hear you.

Every one of these people play a role in ensuring your presentation is a success.

Sometimes things don't go according to plan. Your microphone may stop working half-way through your presentation or you were promised an additional table for your resources and it wasn't set up. Unless it will compromise your presentation in a major way hold off on the tantrum and adjust your expectations. Can it be rectified? Yes! That is super. No? Well, let's see what we can work with here.

From the first contact with the client to the very last evaluation process, be friendly and easy. Send things on time or earlier than expected, forward additional resources to help with the promotion and marketing, offer any help that would ensure the success of the event, be on time and be grateful for the opportunity to present.

Referrals are essential for presenters. Be referred for being a great speaker and a nice guy or girl, not blacklisted for the worst attitude.

Often I have referred the speaker who is professional and a pleasure to deal with rather than the celebrity speaker even if their content was great. This is especially true if I have to share the platform with them too. There is nothing worse than having a miserable and difficult team member.

Other ways you can demonstrate how courteous you are:

- ✓ Wipe down whiteboards after you have used them
- ✓ Leave a training room or platform as you found it
- ✓ Wear the appropriate attire
- ✓ Be available after the presentation
- ✓ Bring your own resources (markers, remote presenter, handouts)
- ✓ Send a thank you card after the event to anyone who went out of their way to help you
- ✓ Keep any promises you have made.

It's the little things that can make a big difference to how people talk about you and your brand way after the audience has gone home.

HAVE A LAUGH

Humour lightens the load

"Humour is the affectionate communication of insight." (Leo Rosten)

There is rarely an occasion where humour is not appropriate at some level.

However, just like beauty is in the eye of the beholder, we don't all agree on what is funny and what is not funny so as a presenter we don't want to get the audience offside by choosing inappropriate humour.

A very safe rule for presenters is: "Don't tell jokes". Jokes are usually designed to offend somebody. It is a red flag you're waving. Regardless of how much research you do about your target audience, you don't really know your audience. You don't know their personal, religious, sexual, cultural and political view or beliefs.

Self-deprecating humour, however, is usually a winner. Not too much, just enough to connect with your audience and to demonstrate that you too can make mistakes and have a laugh about matters that really are trivial compared to the big picture. Too much self-deprecation though may be detrimental to your credibility.

Great humour is off-the-cuff humour relating to the immediate experience or by the re-telling of your funny personal stories and experiences. You may not even be the source of all the humour, you may have a class clown or some very quick-witted attendees. It is still your role to facilitate the humour to ensure it is appropriate.

Another red flag is swearing. I know some presenters get away with it, but some presenters don't mind if they offend the audience either and never get asked back.

Did you know that the study of laughter and its effects on the body is called gelotology? Gelotology was first studied by psychiatrists and doctors really did recommend laughter as a form of medicine, hence the term "Laughter is the best medicine". Laughter requires the coordination of many muscles throughout the body. Laughter increases your blood pressure and heart rate, it changes breathing, reduces levels of some neurochemicals and provides a boost to the immune system. Laughter reduces stress and helps us to relax. It is in this state that our attendees are going to enjoy your presentation and be open to new information and experiences.

The first laughter appears at about 3.5 to 4 months of age, way before we are able to speak. The average adult laughs 17 times a day and it has been suggested that a small child laughs on average 300 times a day. This could be because as they reach four or five they are interacting more with other small children. We as presenters need to give permission to our attendees to have fun and laugh more with their new friends in our room.

Learning should be fun. If you remove the stress from learning and let the laughter in, you will enhance the entire learning experience for everyone, including yourself.

PRACTICE DOESN'T MAKE PERFECT

Script, notes and other useful tips

Practice makes perfect if you are rehearsing a script. Practice doesn't always make perfect when you are going to present, especially if you are practising a less-than-perfect presentation.

Rehearsing is essential but it is very hard to remember every word of a 90-minute presentation let alone a seven-hour workshop. Practice your openings, practice your closings, practice the way you deliver your key messages, practice your stories. In fact, practice your whole presentation several times over, but always be prepared to use not only your subject matter and presenter expertise but also your flexpertise.

I have delivered similar keynotes or trainings programmes, sometimes 100 times or more. I have never ever delivered the exact same talk because I have never had the exact same audience. I need to be so comfortable with my content and presentation that I can be flexible to meet the needs of my audience and client and be adaptable if something just isn't going to plan.

Now for one of the most commonly asked questions I get asked in my presentation skills programmes: How do I remember everything?

Well the answer is: I don't!

Sure, in a 30- or 60-minute presentation when practiced enough I generally remember everything because of the way I have structured my presentation (important learning in that sentence). However, in longer presentations, ones with lots of important facts and figures in them, or in training workshops, I strategically choose my presenter aids and cues.

Now, you are not in high school any more so palm cards are no longer an option but you can have your notes. It's how you use those notes that makes the difference. I recently asked a colleague to take over one of my roles as MC for an association. She was reluctant to do so because she didn't think she could remember all the information and make the witty comments I was delivering every month. I said I didn't think she could remember them either. I always have my notes on the MC lectern. She was very surprised I had notes, and I was surprised she thought I was clever enough to remember multi-speakers' introductions or biographies and hours of agenda items. After a laugh and pep talk she graciously accepted the role.

Place your notes somewhere you have access to them, but if you are presenting not MCing don't use them unless you really need to. If you do have one of those moments and need to glance at your notes (not read them), take the attention away from you by giving the audience something to do while you go and take a peek. If you are using notes, you don't need a word-for-word script, just key words, concepts, phrases, story titles in order on the page. If you are designing a presentation for someone else to deliver then it must be in as much detail as possible; they can then make their own notes once they are comfortable with the content.

A quick tip for the oldies. Each year I seem to print my notes out in a bigger font. Ensure your notes are just key word notes in a large enough font to glance at them.

You can pre-write on flip charts or whiteboards – your audience thinks you have prepared it for them but sometimes it helps to keep you on track. If you have to draw an image, chart or some other wordy information you think you may not remember how to spell, (it's usually the most simple word you forget and your credibility is lost in a split second) – or in my case draw it so badly no-one will know what it is anyway – pre-draw or write it in very light lead pencil. Your audience can't see it and you can just trace around it. Saved!

Your slides can prompt you but do not use your slides as a crutch because if there is a power failure, you may be left standing there with nothing to say, looking like a fool. I always print a copy of all my slides and have them with my notes.

I also place items, props, handouts and other items around the room as triggers to remind me. For example, I have a handout table with everything in order. I check from time to time that the right handout has been given out at the right time. There should be nothing left by the end of the presentation. I can set my remote presenter to vibrate to remind me to do something. I can place coloured posters in order around the room to trigger my memory, also providing visual stimuli for the audience.

If you use a good presentation structure when you are designing your presentation you will find once you are on a roll, each piece of your presentation delivered will be the guide to the next piece, just like remembering a sequence of events.

When you are practising, ensure you are self-reviewing by filming yourself or asking a trusted source to critique you. You should really do both.

Perfect practice makes for a powerful presentation, not practice makes perfect.

FEEDBACK IS CRITICAL FOR GROWTH

Not all feedback will help you grow

All great presenters have coaches and mentors just like business people. Feedback is critical for growth.

Do we take on board all the feedback we get though and how do we know who to listen to?

All feedback is relevant. Why? Because perception is everything. If someone tells you that your presentation was boring, it really was, for them anyway. It doesn't mean that everybody in the audience feels the same way; in fact, they could be the only one that feels this way so find out why it was boring for them rather than changing your whole presentation for no particular reason or going somewhere to rock in the corner because you are so distressed about the negative feedback.

Let's be honest though, negative feedback hurts. Some presenters avoid feedback because they don't know how to handle their emotions when they get some. You must choose trusted sources to give you the type of feedback you want. Have a conversation prior to coach the coach about the type of feedback you are looking for.

You may just want some feedback on a new model you are presenting and whether you managed to make the model simple for everyone to understand, and then at the end of the presentation you get a full presentation critique, from how many ums you did and how you worked the stage to what you decided to wear – from someone who has never presented.

Once the pain has gone from the negative feedback, look at it objectively and decide how much merit the comments have. Then you have the power to choose what to do about it, if anything at all.

Celebrate positive feedback. Again, only if it has come from the right source. My mum, I am sure, will always give me positive feedback. Not quite sure I want to use Mum's loving rose-tinted glasses opinion of me as my measurement of a successful presentation. Not just because she's my mum but I can't imagine she will be handing me a cheque for my presentation any time soon.

Ensure the feedback you get is from the people who count before you make any major changes to the way in which you present or the content you deliver.

If you are delivering a sales presentation, don't just get a speech coach to critique you, get someone who specialises in sales, or wait until the sales figures are in – that is a true indication of your presentation success.

Your authenticity must take the lead here too. They may not love what you wear but it aligns to your signature brand. They may complain how opinionated you are but that is why they booked you in the first place. They may just love everything about you but you just suck as a public speaker.

If you decide you are ready to move your presentation skills to the next level you can practice more, present more, and go and watch other presenters you admire and respect. You may even decide to enrol in a course to get some peer feedback from others going through a similar journey.

Or you can choose a coach or a mentor.

"Most importantly, if you're going to ask (for feedback), be ready to change."

- David Maister

When choosing a coach or a mentor to help you to become a better presenter, ask yourself these questions:

- ✓ What type of feedback do I need?
- ✓ Do we share the same values?
- ✓ What personal experience does this person have and is that important?
- ✓ Do they have any formal qualifications in either the content, presenting or coaching, and does this matter to me?
- ✓ Do they know people who can help with other areas of my business or life?
- ✓ Will they be honest and impartial at all times?
- ✓ Will they let me make all the important decisions rather than pushing their opinions on me?
- ✓ Will they keep me accountable?
- ✓ Will they push me to grow too fast or take me on a journey that is too slow?
- ✓ Is this going to be an enjoyable experience?
- ✓ Do we click? And is this important?

This list is by no means exhaustive. You can add more questions that you think are critical and relevant for your growth as a presenter. Don't just jump in with the first person promising to make you a star and get steered in a direction that isn't right for you. You will find the outcome won't serve you or your presentation goals. Choose one or more coaches that feel right for you for the right reasons.

Enjoy your growth journey.

FIND YOUR TRIBE

Your mates not your market

There are other ways to grow as a presenter, trainer or professional speaker. Hang around others who are doing it – others who have trodden the road before you and are willing to share their experiences with you.

Who are you hanging around? Are these people helping you to grow, develop and be the very best presenter you can be? Who are you learning from? Who are you keen to share a platform with? Who would you like to do a joint venture with?

I have joined many associations over the years to network and hang out with many like-minded souls. I have gained so much from each group. The people, the regular workshops and even the social functions have all firmly placed some special memories in my heart. In fact, I was even a founding committee member of a training association almost 20 years ago which I still regularly attend and speak for.

I stumbled across the National Speakers Association by accident about 5 years ago after running a successful

training and speaking business for many years. Joining the association that very first night was one of the best decisions I have ever made for my growth as a presenter. Now I get to hang out with professional speakers from all over the world. One of the NSAA mantras is "We are your mates not your market". Some of my dearest friends are now professional speakers.

It has been said that you are the sum of the five people you are closest to or spend the most time with. Are you spending time with people who are bringing out the very best in you? People who give you honest and genuine feedback or are happy to celebrate your milestones and success?

I receive so much from being involved in industry associations and hanging around like-minded people. In fact, last year I served as President of the National Speakers Association Western Australian Chapter as a way of giving back to the industry. A few years ago I was also acknowledged by my peers and was awarded my CSP (Certified Speaking Professional) the highest designation of the speaking industry worldwide – a night my speaker friends made so very special for me.

Although I ran a successful training business for many years prior to joining a speaking community, I am now a much more confident, professional and passionate speaker by being around and learning from my speaking tribe and community.

You may not want to join an association, you may just want to network, join in online conversations, go to conferences or seek out new friends who present.

Choose your tribe. Learn from the people in your tribe and always give as much back as you receive so you too can help others to grow.

BE TRANSFORMATIONAL

Not transactional

The one and only reason you have been asked to present is because your message has the power to change the behaviours of those who are attending.

Even if you are presenting your own seminar or training workshop, or pitching for business, your goal is to influence the behaviours of the people listening to your message.

Aim to be a transformational presenter. A transformational presenter is one who cares about the success of everyone in the room. A transformational presenter is one who leads positive change. A transformational presenter inspires people to buy into or follow their mission and message.

Although there is a market for transactional presenters – one who pops in, does a talk and moves on to the next client – a transformational presenter invests time and resources to engage in a much longer mutually beneficial relationship.

If you want to be seen as a transformational presenter you need to make sure you ask for and get the action you intended. You need to ensure your presentation message is designed and delivered in a way which incites the audience to change their thinking and behaviour.

No action, no transformation! Like transformational leadership, if you are presenting you are responsible for leading change.

According to researcher Bernard M Bass there are four component of transformational leadership.

- ✓ Intellectual stimulation
- ✓ Individualised consideration
- ✓ Inspirational motivation
- ✓ Idealised influence

All elements of a powerful presentation.

So what is a motivational speaker? This is a speaker who comes into an organisation to inspire and motivate the audience. Many motivational speakers just deliver a great pep talk. On many occasions in business presentations the main content and the structure of the talk has been greatly influenced by the organisational heads.

According to James MacGregor Burns, transformational leadership is about leaders and followers helping each other to advance to a higher level of morale and motivation.

If you let the audience know throughout your presentation that you are invested in the outcome and their success, you will build rapport and trust with the client and audience.

Transformational presenters are concerned with making a real difference.

ENJOY EVERY MOMENT

You'll leave them wanting more

In my first book *Speaking in the Shower: Presentation Skills Exposed* I discussed the three types of public speakers:

> **The Resisters** – Those who resist any opportunity to speak. First reaction is "Kill me now".

> **The Supporters** – Those who accept speaking is some times necessary to get the job done and may even enjoy it.

> **The Enthusiasts** – Pick me, pick me! Actively seeks opportunities to speak in public.

Many resisters, if given the training and the confidence, can move over quite easily to become a supporter and may even one day be completely converted to becoming an enthusiast.

However, there a quite a few people who truly dislike presenting or public speaking of any kind. That's okay, we can't all like everything. My suggestion is, if you can avoid it without any major consequences, just don't do it. If you have a message for the world there are many other ways of sharing it. Like writing or getting someone else to present for you.

If you do choose to present, ENJOY IT. If you are enjoying the presentation, it will show. If you are passionate and committed to the topic it will show. If you are having fun and you allow your audience to do the same it will be a much more rewarding experience for everyone.

If you are not enjoying your presentations, ask yourself why. You may actually enjoy presenting, but you just may not be enjoying presenting this topic or you may not have a connection with some target groups.

If you are passionate about your message, concerned about the success of everyone in the room and have conquered the nerves of speaking in public you will enjoy every moment on the platform.

I know I have said on many occasions, "It's all about the audience, not you", but if you don't belong on the platform, step aside for someone who does as you are then doing the very best for the audience.

Every speaker also has an ego. As long as it doesn't get in the way of putting your audience first, let your ego enjoy the limelight, the spotlight and any other light that is bestowed upon you.

I liked the first time someone asked me to sign my book. I like it when I receive great feedback. I like it when I get special VIP treatment because I am the speaker. In every job you will have good and bad days and good and bad tasks. Let the good days be a day of celebration and the reward for the tasks you do that you don't always enjoy but are necessary.

If you deliver a dynamic, passionate, enjoyable presentation that gets results you will be asked back as you've just left the audience wanting more.

As quoted by Maya Angelou:

"I've learned that people will forget what you said, people will forget what you did, but people will never forget how you made them feel."

You can add to that – give yourself permission to enjoy the way the audience made you feel.

SELLING FROM THE PLATFORM

Are not dirty words

Presenting really is sales. You are either selling a product, a service, an idea or a concept.

Many presenters say they do not sell from the stage – but they do, every time they take the floor or share their message!

Selling from the platform is a marketing strategy that sales people have been successfully using for many years.

It involves speaking to an audience then offering a product or service for sale at the end of the presentation. Organisations and individuals can use speaking as a business or as a marketing strategy to build business. It can raise your profile, position yourself as an expert or market leader in your industry or it can get you in a room full of potential clients.

Speakers either speak for fee or speak for free. Some like myself do both.

If I am speaking for fee I will never sell from the platform unless I have been given permission to do so. The agreed fee I am receiving is for my presentation or speaking service.

I often speak for free if my target clients are the audience. This gives me the opportunity to put myself in front of potential new clients. If I do a great job they may purchase my services or products or refer me to other clients. Only speak for free if you believe there are potential new client in the audience, you are a less experienced speaker wanting more experience, you are trying out a new keynote and wanting some feedback from a live audience or if you are speaking to a charitable or not for profit organisation and decide to waiver or donate your fee.

Many event organisers state there is no budget for speakers even though they are charging a large fee for participants to attend.

The speakers are the main feature of the event and without them there wouldn't be an event. The event organiser pockets all the profit and you work all day for no return. Not a good business model for you unless, as I mentioned previously, you want to be put in front of this particular audience to showcase yourself, your services and your products.

A selling from the platform model that the seminar industry often uses is inviting people to either a free or low cost seminar to fill a room then once they have built rapport and provided lots of great content they then offer them the next level of product or service. If done with honesty and integrity it is a great marketing strategy that can work for almost every type of business or industry. Many seminar leaders also enter into joint ventures with other providers to provide multi speaker events. The problem with this model is that there are many cases where hundreds or thousands of people are packed in a room thinking they are there to get great content but find themselves seated in a "sales fest" with a lots of people promising the world to them if they just hand over their credit cards.

There are just as many genuine seminar people in the industry too, so

as long as you are comfortable with what is on offer and do not feel you have been pressured into anything you may regret later (although there are cooling off periods) then going to these type of events can be extremely educational and rewarding.

If you are a speaker or business owner who love your products and services and enjoys selling to many instead of one, then becoming a great sell from the platform speaker is just a no brainer. Many professional speakers now make more money from selling their products and services from the platform than they do from their traditional speaking fees.

There are also a variety of online platforms available for this type of marketing strategy now too. You can deliver a free or low cost webinar, an online training programme or even a video series and upsell to your next level of product or service or make another great offer at the end of the presentation. You can even interview some other expert speakers and let each of them promote their offering if they will speak to your clients for no upfront fee.

Selling from the platform are not dirty words if your intention is to serve your audience and do what is best for them. Your products and services may be just what they are searching for.

SPEAK, SPEAK AND SPEAK SOME MORE

Where to find speaking opportunities

To get better at speaking you must speak. Reading the 52 principles in this book will give you a solid introductory understanding of why you need to do or say everything but you will truly learn when you stand up and speak out to a live audience. All theory and no practice will never make you a great or even a good presenter.

Ten thousand hours of practice is the number said before you can call yourself an expert. I am sure many of you will be speaking superstars before that number but if you work towards speaking for 10,000 hours there will be no doubt about your commitment to becoming a powerful presenter.

It is essential to practice your speaking; however, it's not always a good idea to practice in front of that A grade client you have been wanting to close the deal with. So who do you practice on? Non-paying clients is a great idea. There are hundreds if not thousands of non-paying, but very appreciative, audiences just waiting for you to offer to speak to them.

These clients are your business associations, industry associations, community groups, sporting groups, not-for-profit organisations, church groups and even high schools. Not to say all of these groups will never pay you. Many do have budgets for speakers but only charge them or discuss fees when you are comfortable charging them.

You can agree to be interviewed, you can offer to speak for free with other paid speakers so you get to share the platform with some great names or you can decide to offer free talks to your very own clients.

If you are a workplace trainer or presenter see if you can do the first few presentations with an experienced presenter or a mentor before you are ready to go it alone.

Many presenters avoid speaking until they are convinced they are ready to go to market. You will never get any better if you don't have the opportunity to practice in front of a live audience. Remember though, perfect practice not practice makes perfect. Practice builds confidence and allows you to see what is working and what isn't so you can craft a superb presentation and finally deliver it to that A grade client you have been waiting for.

If you are charging for your speaking services make sure you do not undervalue the services you are offering. Yes, professional speakers seem to get paid a very good remuneration by the hour, but you have had to do all the design, preparation and consultation before the presentation. And you may own the IP. All these charges must be considered when invoicing. Don't forget to charge on the basis of the value you are bringing not by the hour. Million Dollar Consulting by Alan Weiss is another must read if you are ever in doubt about your fee for speaking.

So don't shy away from speaking opportunities – the more speaking you do the more speaking opportunities will come your way.

BE PASSIONATE ABOUT YOUR PACKAGE

Protect your reputation and brand

Every presenter has a personal brand. You don't get to choose. And it's judged by your audience, your clients, your peers and your potential clients.

You need to be in charge of your brand or others will be managing it for you. And you might not like how it is being done.

In Principle 18 we talked about being your authentic self, being the expert in being you. This is your brand. Your brand must be a reflection of who you really are. It must be based on your personality, your values, your strengths, your vision and your brand promise.

Your brand promise is a commitment to your clients and your audience. A commitment that states every time you do business with them, they will get exactly what is promised. The experience will be consistent, it will add value to them and you will never make promises that you will not keep.

If you keep changing your brand or your brand promise your market will be confused. For example, if you always wear casual attire, then you rock up to a presentation or two in a three-piece suit or you are known for playing music throughout all of your presentations but then decide not to do it on this one occasion. Your client or audience will feel like you have broken a promise to them and that damages the relationship.

Your personal brand is not your designer suit or fancy tie. It's not your flashy stationery or your funky new office. All of these items must align to your brand but they are not your brand. Your brand is you. Your brand is your promise. Your brand is your whole package.

The package consists of your image, your competencies, your uniqueness, your values and how you build and nurture your relationships.

Once you decide what brand to build you must decide on what strategies you will employ to market and protect your brand.

Your brand is like your reputation. It can take years to build and two minutes to damage. One wrong move on a social media site or in the press could cost you the years of hard work building and protecting your brand.

Be mindful of doing business or sharing the platform with others who do not align with the image or values of your brand. You will be judged, whether you believe it to be right or wrong, on the people you hang out with or seem to be doing business with.

Always stay passionate about your package. It's the only one you really have.

PRINCIPLES HAVEN'T REALLY CHANGED IN 2,000 YEARS

Presenters have always been powerful educators and leaders

Very often we are public speaking without knowing we are doing it – telling a story, sharing an experience or teaching someone to do something new. Perhaps it should have been called public sharing.

If we look back at history some of the most powerful influencers in the world were the people who had the courage to share.

The art of public speaking was first developed by the ancient Greeks. Greek orators spoke on their own behalf rather than on behalf of others. If citizens wished to succeed in court, politics or social life they needed to learn the techniques of public speaking.

In classical Greece and Rome, the main component was rhetoric (that is, composition and delivery of speeches). Aristotle was credited with developing the basic system of the art of rhetoric (study of persuasion) dating from the 4th century BC and his treatise Rhetoric is regarded by most rhetoricians as the most important single work on persuasion ever written.

Aristotle's work defines three modes of persuasion:

Ethos – Character (today we talk about the credibility of the speaker based on their knowledge, values, beliefs, expertise)

Pathos – Suffering or experience, appealing to or awakening to one's emotions (today we talk about being emotionally relevant)

Logos – The argument (today we talk about evidence presented in a logical sequence)

And his teachings go on to talk about rhythm, style, deliberate language, and figurative speech.

Over the course of history, storytellers and public speakers began to arise as very important figures in our communities. Shakespeare permanently made his mark on literature as did modern day Steve Jobs with his ability to craft a narrative and always kept the audience in the palm of his hand due to his compelling storytelling.

The principles haven't really changed at all over time. Have we simplified them or made them more complex? You decide.

From long before recorded history to modern day 2014, one message has never been lost.

If you can master powerful presentation principles, you will always make your message matter.

ABOUT THE AUTHOR

Dynamic, infectious, inspiring and passionate are all words that have been used by Paula's clients to describe her as a presenter and trainer.

Author of the books *Speaking in the Shower: Presentation Skills Exposed*, and now *Powerful Presentation Principles*, Paula is a leading authority on standing up and speaking out and specialises in developing exceptional presenters and trainers. Paula was also the developer of Australia's first Presentation Skills Diploma qualification.

Paula was awarded CSP (Certified Speaking Professional) designation by the National Speakers Association of Australia in 2011, the highest possible designation held by only a small number of professional speakers worldwide.

Apart from speaking and training, Paula has been actively engaged in small business and industry for nearly three decades and brings this invaluable experience to her sessions. Her many roles have included director/owner of Australia's largest personal development school, franchisor, hotel owner, training college director, professional speaker, coach and consultant.

Paula's expertise includes: Presentation skills, speaker training and coaching, personal branding and self-leadership.

Her passion is challenging individuals to be the brilliant self-leaders they were born to be.

Apart from a busy speaking and training schedule, Paula is often sought after as a trusted business coach and mentor.

Paula is also a proud mum of three, wife of one and friend to a few more.

You can contact Paula personally by visiting **www.paulasmith.com.au**

"People hear you on the level you speak from.
Speak from your heart,
and they will hear with theirs."

–Marianne Williamson

www.ingramcontent.com/pod-product-compliance
Lightning Source LLC
Chambersburg PA
CBHW081818200326
41597CB00023B/4297